HOME ECONOMICS REVISION
NOTES FOR
JUNIOR CERTIFICATE

MARY ANNE HALTON

GILL & MACMILLAN

Gill & Macmillan Ltd
Goldenbridge
Dublin 8
with associated companies throughout the world
© Mary Anne Halton 1997
0 7171 2501 7
Print origination in Ireland by Sally O'Leary

CONTENTS

SOCIAL AND HEALTH STUDIES

TEXTILE STUDIES

PREPARING FOR THE EXAM

EXAM PAPERS

1

NUTRITION AND DIET

FOOD CHOICES

WHAT IS FOOD?

Food is any solid or liquid which provides nutrients (protein, fats, carbohydrates, vitamins, minerals, water) for the growth, activity and functioning of the human body.

REASONS FOR EATING FOOD

- To help the growth and repair of body cells
- To provide fuel for our bodies which is converted into heat and energy
- To provide protection against disease
- To regulate body temperature, breathing, digestion and other body functions

We also eat because:
- We enjoy eating
- We like different foods, their flavour and their smell
- We like eating with other people
- We enjoy celebrating special events in our lives
- Food advertising might make us feel hungry

FACTORS AFFECTING FOOD CHOICES AND EATING HABITS

- Special dietary requirements
- Parents
- Family budget
- Cultural or religious background
- Age
- Friends
- Advertising
- Where we live (city, countryside, island, etc.)
- Availability of different foods
- Knowledge of healthy eating
- Likes and dislikes
- Lifestyle or social life

SOME DEFINITIONS

ANAEMIA results from a lack of iron in the diet.

A BALANCED DIET is one which contains a variety of foods which provide us with nutrients in their correct proportions.

BASAL METABOLIC RATE is the least amount of energy we need when our body is resting to keep it functioning.

BERIBERI is a disease which affects nerve pulses. Lack of thiamine causes beriberi.

CHOLESTEROL is a hard substance (sterol) which is produced in the body and is found in some foods of animal origin.

DEFICIENCY SYMPTOMS result from a lack of, or a reduced intake or poor absorption of, nutrients.

ELEMENTS are the basic building blocks of each nutrient. Examples of elements are carbon, hydrogen and oxygen.

EMPTY KILOCALORIES are produced by alcohol, biscuits, cakes, crisps and sweets.

EMULSIONS are formed when oil and water or vinegar are mixed vigorously together (French dressing, mayonnaise). Emulsions can be temporary or permanent.

ENERGY is described as 'the ability to do work'. Energy is produced in the body from the foods we eat.

ENZYMES are chemical substances which cause a chemical reaction without changing themselves, as in the maturation of fruit or digestion of food.

FORTIFIED FOODS are foods to which nutrients have been added. Examples are bread, breakfast cereals, super milk, TVP and white flour.

FUNCTIONS are what the various nutrients found in food do for the body.

GOITRE results from an insufficient amount of iodine in the diet, causing the thyroid gland to swell.

HAEMOGLOBIN is a protein found in blood. It picks up oxygen and carries it to the body cells.

MACRO-NUTRIENTS are protein, fat and carbohydrate. They have a large structure which must be broken down by chemical activity in the digestive system before they can be absorbed.

MALNUTRITION results from an imbalance of nutrients in the diet. This imbalance causes deficiency diseases. Some people in the world do not have enough to eat and suffer from deficiency diseases and starvation. Other people eat a lot of the wrong types of foods because they make poor food choices. Malnutrition can occur in both cases.

METABOLIC RATE is the rate at which our bodies use up energy.

MICRO-NUTRIENTS are vitamins and minerals. They are smaller in structure than the macro-nutrients.

NUTRITIONISTS are people who study food and apply the knowledge they have acquired to help people develop healthy eating habits, balanced diets and in some cases special diets.

OBESITY is the term used when a person is overweight (weight is not in proportion to height).

OSTEOMALACIA is a bone disease in adults, similar to rickets in children.

OXIDATION is the process whereby energy is released from food by the body. In the cells, oxygen combines with food to produce energy.

REFINED FOODS are foods that have been processed commercially and the cellulose removed (such as flour, packet soups, white bread, white rice).

RICKETS is a bone disease in children caused by a deficiency of vitamin D/ calcium/phosphorus.

STAPLE FOODS are the foods which are readily available and used frequently in a country (such as potatoes in Ireland, pasta in Italy, rice in Thailand). They are the foods traditionally used in that country.

WHOLE CEREALS are cereals which do not have the outer layer removed.

NUTRIENTS

WHAT IS A NUTRIENT?

A nutrient is a complex chemical substance found in food. Nutrients are essential for the functioning of our bodies.

Six constituents are found in food, of which five are nutrients:

i	PROTEINS	iv	VITAMINS
ii	FATS	v	MINERALS
iii	CARBOHYDRATES	vi	WATER (a constituent but not a nutrient)

Nutrients are divided into two groups:

i **MACRO-NUTRIENTS**   ii **MICRO-NUTRIENTS**
(proteins, fats, carbohydrates)   (minerals, vitamins)

PROTEINS

Amino acids:
The basic protein unit is an amino acid. Each amino acid is made up of elements. Amino acids join together to form chains of larger protein units.

The elements found in protein:

CARBON • **HYDROGEN** • **OXYGEN** • **NITROGEN**

HBV/LBV	
CLASS/TYPE	SOURCE
HBV/ANIMAL	Fish, meat, milk, cheese, eggs, soya beans (exception)
LBV/VEGETABLE	Pulses (peas, beans, lentils), cereals, nuts, potatoes, pasta

What are HBV and LBV?
    HBV: High biological value (mainly animal sources)
    LBV: Low biological value (mainly vegetable sources)

Functions of protein:
- Produces heat and energy
- Growth and repair of cells
- Production of antibodies, enzymes and hormones

Effects of protein deficiency:
- Stunted growth
- Cells slow to repair
- Fewer antibodies produced
- Imbalance in hormones and enzymes

Recommended dietary allowance (RDA):
    1 gram protein per 1 kilo of body weight.

Energy produced:
    1 gram protein = 4 kcal/17kJ

Current dietary guidelines:
 It is recommended that the balanced daily diet should be made up
 of animal and vegetable protein.

FATS
....

Fats are one of our concentrated energy foods. Fats also add flavour to our
foods. Fats are made up of:

 FATTY ACIDS ● GLYCEROL

SOURCES OF FAT	
CLASSES/TYPES	**SOURCES**
SATURATED (mainly animal)	Milk, cream, cheese, butter, eggs, meat, lard, suet, meat products (sausages)
UNSATURATED (mainly vegetable)	Nuts, whole cereals, pulses, oily fish, vegetable cooking oils, polyunsaturated margarine/spreads

The elements found in fats:
 CARBON ● HYDROGEN ● OXYGEN

Functions of fat:
 ● Produces heat and energy
 ● Provides insulation for the body underneath the skin
 ● Provides a source of the fat-soluble vitamins A, D, E and K
 ● Kidneys, nerves and delicate organs are protected with a layer of fat.
   This layer can prevent damage to organs, e.g. in accidents

Effects of fat deficiency:
 Deficiency of fat is very rare.

Recommended dietary allowance (RDA):
 As deficiency is unusual, there is no RDA.

Energy produced:
 1 gram fat = 9 kcals/34kJ

Current dietary guidelines:
 Dietary guidelines recommend that people should eat less saturated
 fats and more vegetable fats. Saturated fats are high in cholesterol.

Foods containing fats also supply fat-soluble vitamins, so fats should not be excluded totally from the diet.
Low-fat foods are unsuitable for babies.

CARBOHYDRATES

Carbohydrates are one of our energy foods. The process which produces carbohydrates is called photosynthesis. Sugars are the most basic form of carbohydrate.

The elements found in carbohydrates:

CARBON ● HYDROGEN ● OXYGEN

Functions of carbohydrate:
- Provides heat and energy
- Dietary fibre helps the movement of food along the digestive system (peristalsis)
- Dietary fibre helps to prevent constipation
- Excess carbohydrate is converted into fat, which insulates the body (adipose tissue)
- Helps reduce incidence of bowel disease

SOURCES OF CARBOHYDRATE	
CLASSES	SOURCES
DIETARY FIBRE	Fruits, vegetables, whole cereals (skins and husks), wholemeal brown bread, brown rice
STARCH	Potatoes, root and pulse vegetables, rice, pasta, cereals, flour, bread
SUGAR	Soft drinks, sweets, biscuits, cakes, sugar, milk, fresh and dried fruit, honey

Effects of carbohydrate deficiency:
Carbohydrate foods are generally the most plentiful of all foods. Deficiency is rare.

Energy produced:
1 gram carbohydrate = 4 kcal/17kj

Current dietary guidelines:
Dietary guidelines recommend that we choose more dietary fibres and starches than sugars. Avoid foods that are mainly sugar.
We should increase our intake of fruit and vegetables.

DIETARY FIBRE

Dietary fibre is important in our daily diet. Fibre-rich foods are plentiful and reasonably cheap.

Sources:
Fibre is only present in foods of plant origin. Processed, convenience and refined foods are low in fibre or lack fibre.

Functions of dietary fibre:
- Prevents constipation because of the way it provides bulk in our diet
- Absorbs water and makes us feel full
- Picks up chemicals and toxins as it passes along the intestine and these are eliminated in the faeces
- Encourages peristalsis
- Fibre-rich foods provide vitamin B, which helps the release of energy in the body

Problems associated with low-fibre diets:
- Constipation
- Diverticulosis
- Haemorrhoids

Recommended dietary allowance (RDA):
The RDA for dietary fibre is 30g per day.

MICRO-NUTRIENTS

The two micro-nutrients are minerals and vitamins.

MINERALS

The body needs minerals in smaller amounts than the other nutrients. Examples of minerals include calcium, iron, iodine, sodium, potassium, phosphorus, zinc and fluorine. Some minerals need certain vitamins to be present so that they work efficiently in the body.

Trace elements:
These are minerals which the body needs in much smaller amounts, e.g. zinc and iodine.

CALCIUM

Food sources:
Calcium is present in dairy foods (milk, cheese, yoghurt), eggs, tinned fish (bones), green vegetables and white flour (fortified).

Functions of calcium:
- Healthy teeth, bones, nerves and muscles
- Assists the clotting of blood

Effects of deficiency:
- Poor bones and teeth
- Osteoporosis (adults)
- Rickets (children)

Calcium combines with phosphorus to make bones and teeth hard and strong. Calcium and phosphorus need vitamin D to be present in the diet so that they may be absorbed properly.

IRON

Food sources:
Iron is found in lean red meat, offal (liver, kidneys), dark green vegetables (cabbage), wholegrain cereals, wholemeal bread and sardines.

Functions of iron:
Iron is needed for the formation and functioning of healthy red blood cells.

Effects of deficiency:
- Anaemia
- Feeling tired, no energy

IODINE

Food sources:
Iodine is found in seaweed (carrageen moss), sea fish, cereals, vegetables and sea salt.

Functions of iodine:
- Formation of thyroxine
- Functioning of the thyroid gland

Effects of deficiency:
- Overweight and tiredness
- Goitre

PHOSPHORUS

Phosphorus works with calcium to develop strong bones and teeth. Vitamin D is needed for its absorption.

Food sources:
Phosphorus is found in dairy foods (milk, cheese), meat, poultry, fish, eggs, whole cereals and pulse vegetables.

Functions of phosphorus:
Phosphorus is needed for healthy, strong bones and teeth.

Effects of deficiency:
None known, as phosphorus is available from a wide variety of foods.

POTASSIUM

Food sources:
Potassium is found in meat, milk, dark green vegetables, bananas and citrus fruits.

Functions of potassium:
Helps the functioning of cells and muscles.

Effects of deficiency:
As potassium is found in a variety of foods, deficiency rarely occurs.

SODIUM

Food sources:
Sodium is found in snack foods, such as crisps, salted nuts, table salt and bacon rashers.

Functions of sodium:
- Helps to regulate the water balance in the body
- Important for the functioning of cells

Effects of deficiency:
Cramps in muscles.

VITAMINS

Vitamins are classified into two groups:
- Fat-soluble vitamins: A, D, E and K
- Water-soluble vitamins: B group and C

FAT-SOLUBLE VITAMINS

VITAMIN A

Food sources:
- Dairy foods (milk, cheese, butter), margarine, liver, fish liver oils, eggs
- Carotene, found in carrots, oranges and tomatoes (in the body, carotene can be converted into vitamin A)

Functions of vitamin A:
- Healthy lining membranes (throat and nose)
- Growth
- Healthy eyes and skin

Effects of deficiency:
- Dry lining membranes
- Dry skin
- Retarded growth
- Night blindness

VITAMIN D

Vitamin D can be produced by the action of sunlight on the skin. We also get vitamin D from food sources. Vitamin D helps the absorption of calcium in the body.

Food sources:
Vitamin D is found in oily fish, cod liver oil, liver, eggs, margarine and dairy products (cheese).

Functions of vitamin D:
- Formation of healthy bones and teeth
- Prevents rickets

Effects of deficiency:
- Rickets (bone disease in children)
- Dental problems

VITAMIN K

Vitamin K is found in food. It is also manufactured in the body.

Food sources:
Vegetables, liver, cereals, fish.

Functions of vitamin K:
Essential for the clotting of the blood.

Effects of deficiency:
Blood does not clot properly.

WATER-SOLUBLE VITAMINS

VITAMIN B GROUP

There are many vitamins in this group. They share similar features but differ in their chemical structure. Some vitamin B is made in the body. Examples of B-group vitamins are thiamine, nicotinic acid and folic acid.

Food sources:
Vitamin B is found in dairy foods (milk, cheese), meat, fish, eggs, wholegrain cereals, wholemeal bread, yeast, pulse vegetables and nuts.

Functions of vitamin B:
- Required for a healthy nervous system
- Helps the release of energy from foods

Effects of deficiency:
- Tiredness and irritability
- Beriberi
- Pellagra

VITAMIN C
Food sources:
Vitamin C is found in fresh fruit (citrus, blackcurrants, rose-hip syrup) and vegetables (peppers, potatoes).

Functions of vitamin C:
- Necessary for general good health
- Builds strong bones and teeth
- Keeps the gums, skin, lining membranes and blood vessels healthy
- Helps form connective tissue
- Aids the absorption of iron
- Prevents scurvy

Effects of deficiency:
- Scurvy
- Wounds take longer to heal
- Iron is not absorbed properly

WATER

Water is essential for life. It is present in every organ of the body. The elements found in water are hydrogen and oxygen. The kidneys regulate the water balance in the body. The human body is about 70% water. Most foods contain some water; some foods have a higher water content than others.

Sources:
   Beverages (tea, milk), water, fruits, vegetables, most foods.

Functions of water:
   ● Quenches thirst
   ● Necessary for healthy body fluids and tissues
   ● Transports nutrients around the body
   ● Transports oxygen and hormones around the body
   ● Needed for waste removal
   ● Source of minerals, e.g. calcium and fluorine
   ● Helps metabolism (digestion and absorption of food)
   ● Regulates body temperature

ENERGY

WHAT IS ENERGY?

Energy is defined as the ability to do work. We need energy for each body function, when resting and when involved in any activity.

WHY DO WE NEED ENERGY?

We need energy for:
   ● Every action that we take
   ● Chemical reactions within our bodies
   ● Muscle and nerve movement
   ● Growth and repair of cells
   ● Maintaining the correct body temperature (37°C)

The food we eat supplies energy. During the process of oxidation, energy is released from food.

MEASURING ENERGY

Energy is measured in kilocalories (kcal) or kilojoules (kJ). 1 kcal = 4.2 kJ

ENERGY NEEDS

The amount of energy we require depends on:
- Body size (height and weight)
- Age (younger people usually need more energy foods)
- Gender (women generally need less energy foods than men)
- Activity (the more active a person is, the more energy they need)
- Climate (generally people living in colder climates need more energy)
- Pregnancy (pregnant and nursing women need more energy foods)

ENERGY BALANCE

> ### ENERGY INTAKE = ENERGY OUTPUT

If we eat more energy foods than we need, the energy produced is converted into and stored as fat.

If we eat too few energy foods, we can suffer from some deficiency disorders.

If we eat a balanced diet, energy intake will be equal to energy output.

A HEALTHY BALANCED DIET

A healthy balanced diet is one which contains all the nutrients in the correct proportions. Foods should be selected from the different food groups. A healthy balanced diet also takes into consideration special dietary needs of individual groups, e.g. diabetics.

TABLE OF DAILY KILOCALORIE NEEDS

PEOPLE		KILOCALORIES PER DAY
Toddlers	(1–3yrs)	1300
Children	(4–6yrs)	1700
	(7–10yrs)	2000
Adolescent boys		2800
Adolescent girls		2300
Active male		2900–3500
Sedentary male		2500–2600
Active female		2500
Sedentary female		2200
Pregnant mother		2400
Nursing mother		2700

HEALTHY EATING GUIDELINES

CURRENT DIETARY GUIDELINES RECOMMEND THAT WE:

- **Eat a variety of foods:** choose foods from the various food groups each day (eat the correct amount from each food group)

- **Increase intake of:** **iron-rich foods** (especially teenage girls and women)
  calcium-rich foods (especially teenage girls and women)
  fibre-rich foods
- **Reduce intake of:** **fat** (especially animal or saturated fat). Do not eliminate fat from the diet completely as it is a source of fat-soluble vitamins.
  salt, when eating food and in the preparation and cooking of food
  sugar in the diet

- **HOW TO INCREASE IRON**

Choose from: Lean red meat, offal (liver, kidneys), dark green vegetables (cabbage), wholegrain cereals, wholemeal bread, sardines.

- **HOW TO INCREASE CALCIUM**

Choose from: Dairy foods (milk, cheese, yoghurt), eggs, tinned fish (bones), green vegetables, white flour (fortified).

- **HOW TO INCREASE DIETARY FIBRE**

Choose from: Fruit, vegetables, whole cereals (skins and husks), wholemeal brown bread, brown rice, high-fibre breakfast cereals. Increase fibre when cooking by choosing fibre-rich ingredients and modifying recipes accordingly.

HOW TO REDUCE FAT – BUT DO NOT LEAVE IT OUT COMPLETELY

- Choose low-fat butters and margarines
- Use spreads and butters sparingly on bread and potatoes
- Choose lean meats
- Remove excess fat when preparing meat
- Drain off excess fat when cooking food
- Eat more pulse vegetables, fish and poultry
- Choose low-fat dairy products (milk, cheese, yoghurt)
- Choose low-fat methods of cooking (grilling, poaching, boiling, baking, stir frying)
- Use vegetable oils rather than hard saturated fats (measure oils carefully)
- Avoid using fried foods every day (e.g. chips) – cook them once a week
- Do not use cooking oil indefinitely in deep-fat fryers – change the oil regularly
- Drain all fried foods on kitchen paper

– Reduce your intake of chocolate, high-fat sugary snacks, crisps, biscuits, cakes, sausages, peanuts, pastries, mayonnaise and cream

- **HOW TO REDUCE SUGAR**

Choose from: Low-sugar or sugar-free foods (fresh fruit), unsweetened fruit juices, low-sugar breakfast cereals. Reduce sugar at table, in beverages and when cooking.

Reduce intake of: Sugary snacks, biscuits, cakes, fizzy drinks, high-sugar breakfast cereals, chocolates, sweets, tinned fruit in syrup.

EXAMPLES OF MODERN DIETARY PROBLEMS

- Coronary heart disease
- High blood pressure
- Obesity
- Tooth decay
- Digestive problems
- Cancer (e.g. cancer of the colon)
- Skin problems

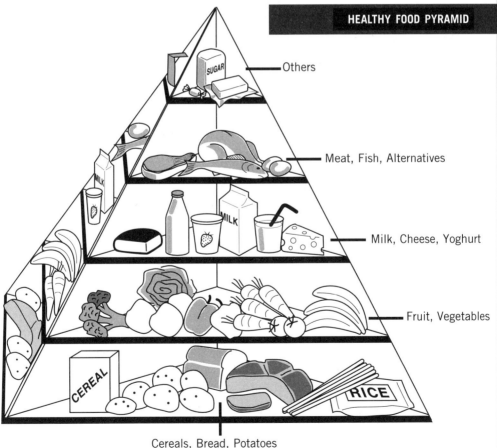

HEALTHY FOOD PYRAMID

Others

Meat, Fish, Alternatives

Milk, Cheese, Yoghurt

Fruit, Vegetables

Cereals, Bread, Potatoes

The four main food groups provide a healthy, varied, balanced diet. All the essential nutrients are present.

RECOMMENDED DAILY SERVINGS FROM THE FOOD GROUPS	
FOOD GROUPS	**SERVINGS**
Cereals, bread and potatoes	6+
Fruit and vegetables	4+
Milk, cheese and yoghurt	3+
Meat, fish and alternatives	2+
Others: fats, oils, sugars, snack foods, alcohol	Sparingly

Alternatives include cheese, eggs, pulses and nuts. **Avoid too many processed and refined foods.**

ALTERNATIVES TO HIGH-SUGAR, HIGH-SATURATED FAT, LOW-FIBRE FOODS	
REPLACE	**WITH**
Crisps	Apple, yoghurt
Fizzy drinks	Fresh unsweetened fruit juice
Pastry	High-fibre pastry
Cream	Natural yoghurt
Chocolate bars	Fresh fruit, yoghurt
Sugary cereals	Porridge
Biscuits	Crackers, unsalted nuts
White rice	Brown rice
White bread	Wholemeal brown bread
White flour	Wholemeal flour
Sugar	Sugar alternative
Burgers	Fish
Cheddar cheese	Low-fat cheddar cheese
Pasta	Wholewheat pasta
Shortcrust pastry	Wholemeal pastry

MODIFYING A RECIPE

WHY RECIPES ARE MODIFIED

- To cater for people on special diets (such as coeliac, vegan)
- To reduce the amount of fat, salt and sugar, and to increase fibre so that it fits into the latest dietary guidelines
- To vary the recipe or if an ingredient is not available, another is substituted
- To make use of leftovers

GENERAL GUIDELINES FOR MODIFYING A RECIPE
- Change one ingredient each time the recipe is used and observe the flavour, texture and appearance of the dish
- Core ingredients are difficult to change in bread, cakes and pastries
- Watch the proportions between ingredients and weigh ingredients accurately
- Make notes on the quantities used

For special diets (e.g. coeliac, diabetes) follow the specific guidelines given by the doctor.

2

INDIVIDUAL DIETARY NEEDS

Groups with individual dietary needs are:
- Babies
- Children
- Adolescents/teenagers
- Adults
- Pregnant or nursing mothers
- Elderly people
- Invalids and convalescents
- People with special dietary needs

BABIES

This is a period of rapid growth.

DIETARY GUIDELINES

0–4 months:
- For the first few months (or until the baby reaches 6 kg in weight) milk is the perfect food, especially breast milk. It has the correct balance of nutrients at the perfect temperature.
- If breast-feeding is not possible, instant infant formula milk is a suitable alternative (ensure that it suits the baby)
- Babies are born with a six-month supply of iron

From about 4/5 months:
- Breast- or bottle-feed
- When the baby is being weaned, suitable foods include baby rice, puréed soups, puréed vegetables, gravy, puréed fruits
- Avoid wheat-based cereals until the baby is about 6 months old

From 5–8 months:
- Breast- or bottle-feed
- Boiled egg yolk
- Puréed or sieved fish or meat with sieved vegetables
- Mashed soft fruits (banana, etc.)

From 8 months:
- Scrambled or boiled egg
- Sieved fish, meat or poultry
- Cooked fruits and vegetables
- Pastas and rice
- Milk as a beverage and in dishes (milk puddings, etc.)
- Yoghurt
- Fruit juice
- Fresh fruit (small pieces)
- Wholemeal bread and toast
- Grated cheese
- Breakfast cereal (suitable for age)

Avoid: Salt, sugar and spicy, fried or fatty foods (difficult to digest).

By one year a baby can eat most food, provided that it is cut into very small pieces. Nutrients essential in a baby's diet include protein, fat, carbohydrate, iron, calcium, vitamin C and dietary fibre.

CHILDREN

Growth is rapid but not as rapid as in the first year. Children are very active and need a good supply of energy foods.

DIETARY GUIDELINES

Choose:
- Protein foods for growth, repair and body building (meat, fish, poultry, eggs, cheese, pulse vegetables, milk, milk products)
- Calcium-rich foods for strong bones and teeth (milk, yogurt, cheese, eggs, green vegetables)
- Carbohydrate foods for energy (wholemeal bread, potatoes, pasta, rice, vegetables, fruit, low-sugar breakfast cereals)

- Vitamin- and mineral-rich foods to protect against disease (fruit, fruit juice, raw and cooked vegetables)
- Choose a wide variety of fresh foods to ensure a healthy balanced diet

Avoid:
- Sweets and biscuits as snacks between meals
- Eating between main meals
- Highly spiced, salty and fatty foods
- Large portions on children's plates
- Too many biscuits, cakes and snack foods (crisps, etc.)
- Rushing family meals

Encourage:
- Regular meal times
- Fruit as a snack between meals
- Good eating habits

ADOLESCENTS/TEENAGERS

This is a period of great change and rapid growth. Extra protein and energy foods are needed to support this growth and activity.

DIETARY GUIDELINES

Choose:
- Energy-rich foods for the increased energy needs of this group (wholemeal bread, cereals, potatoes, pasta, fruit, fruit juice)
- High-fibre foods (whole cereals, wholemeal bread, fruits and vegetables)
- Protein foods for the rapid growth of teenagers
- Vitamins and mineral-rich foods (fruits, vegetables, juices)
- Calcium is needed for developing strong bones and teeth. Teenage girls need a higher intake of iron-rich foods because menstruation results in iron loss.

Avoid:
- Empty kilocalorie foods (crisps, fizzy drinks)
- Fast foods on a daily basis (chips, pizza, burgers)
- Too many sweets or chocolates
- High-sugar, high-fat foods (biscuits)
- Fatty or greasy foods

Encourage:
- Regular meals and healthy snacks
- Yoghurt or fruit as a snack between meals
- Breakfast before going to school
- Healthy balanced mid-morning snacks and packed lunches for school
- Fruit juices instead of tea or coffee

ADULTS

At this stage most people have finished growing. Nutritional requirements are changing and depend on the amount of activity in one's life.

DIETARY GUIDELINES

Choose:
- Protein-rich foods for growth and repair of body cells, manufacture of hormones, enzymes and antibodies
- Energy-rich foods which will provide the right amount of energy for the activities of the adult. Energy intake must equal energy output (excess energy will be converted into fat and the adult could become obese). Manual workers will need a higher intake of energy foods than sedentary workers.
- Vitamin-, mineral- and fibre-rich foods
- Iron-rich foods if you are female (wholemeal bread, lean red meat, liver)

Avoid:
- High-fat, high-sugar foods
- Low-fibre foods
- Too many saturated fats
- Too much salt and salty foods
- Fried foods

PREGNANT OR NURSING MOTHERS

DIETARY GUIDELINES

During pregnancy a woman's need for most nutrients and energy is increased, but she is not eating for two adults. A varied, concentrated diet is important.
Choose:
- Concentrated protein foods for the developing baby
- Dietary fibre to help avoid constipation

- Calcium and vitamin D-rich foods to help the baby develop strong bones and blood (some foods, such as milk, are fortified with vitamins and calcium)
- Iron-rich and vitamin C-rich foods, as some pregnant women suffer from anaemia

When a woman is breast-feeding she needs a diet rich in protein, calcium, iron and energy foods. She should also drink lots of water.

Limit intake of:
- Spicy and fatty foods
- Fried foods
- Sugar-rich foods

Avoid:
- Alcohol
- Cook–chill products
- Soft unpasteurised cheeses

THE ELDERLY

DIETARY GUIDELINES

Choose:
- Nutritionally concentrated foods
- Foods rich in protein, dietary fibre, vitamins and minerals
- Foods rich in calcium, iron and vitamins C and D
- Low-energy foods
- Fortified foods
- Small portions
- Easy-to-digest foods

Avoid:
- Fried, fatty and spicy foods (hard to digest)
- Foods that are difficult to chew
- Foods that are difficult to prepare

INVALIDS AND CONVALESCENTS

DIETARY GUIDELINES

Follow the doctor's advice.
Choose:
- Low-energy foods

- Concentrated protein, vitamin C and iron to assist the recovery of the invalid
- A wide variety of fresh foods which can be prepared simply
- Fruit juice and water as beverages
- Lightly cooked foods

Avoid:
- Fatty and spicy foods
- Fried foods and reheated foods
- Heavy foods (cream cakes, etc.)

VEGETARIANS

Vegetarians are people who choose not to eat meat for moral, religious or other personal reasons.

TYPES OF VEGETARIAN

Lacto-vegetarians do not eat meat, poultry or fish.

Food sources for lacto-vegetarians:
Some foods of animal origin – milk, milk products (cheese, yoghurt, butter), eggs – and fruit, vegetables, nuts, cereals.
It is easy to plan a balanced diet for lacto-vegetarians, as they can eat a wide variety of foods.

Vegans are very strict about their diet. Vegans do not eat any foods or food products that come from animals.

Food sources for vegans:
Vegetables, fruit, nuts, cereals.
A balanced diet for a vegan requires careful planning, as the range of food they eat is limited.

Vegetarians, especially vegans, must read all food labels carefully to avoid foods of animal origin.

DIETARY GUIDELINES FOR VEGETARIANS

Choose:
- Foods that combine a healthy balance of nutrients

- Good sources of vegetable protein in the case of vegans (pulse vegetables, nuts, cereals, soya milk and soya products)
- Protein-rich foods from vegetable sources and foods of animal origin in the case of lacto-vegetarians (milk, cheese, yoghurt, eggs)
- Fibre-rich foods (wholemeal bread, potatoes, nuts, pulse vegetables)
- Vegetable stock or water for soups, sauces, vegetable stews
- Fresh fruit and vegetables for supplies of vitamin C, dietary fibre and other vitamins and minerals
- Yeast extracts, whole cereals, pulse vegetables and potatoes as a good source of B-group vitamins
- Vegetables, cereals, nuts, soya products, as sources of calcium for vegans (add foods from animal origin as sources of calcium for lacto-vegetarians)
- Nuts, vegetables, fruit, wholemeal bread and tofu for iron
- Vegetable oils and fats when frying

COELIACS

Coeliacs are people who are unable to break down foods that contain gluten. Gluten is a protein found in wheat, oats, rye and barley.

The lining of the small intestine can be damaged if coeliacs eat these cereals, or foods made from these cereals. This can result in anaemia and diarrhoea. Stunted growth may also occur.

DIETARY GUIDELINES

- Choose gluten-free foods and food products
- Read all food labels carefully
- Look for the gluten-free symbol on food products
- Choose from meat, poultry, fish, milk, milk products, fruit, vegetables and rice

Avoid:
- Convenience foods unless they display the gluten-free symbol
- Wheat, oats, rye, barley or products made from them (cakes, biscuits, sauces, soups, sausages, etc.)
- Stuffings, coated fish, pasta, spaghetti, batter, potato croquettes

DIABETICS

A diabetic is a person whose pancreas does not produce sufficient insulin to convert glucose into energy. In the case of diabetes, glucose enters the bloodstream and is eliminated from the body in the urine.

TYPES OF DIABETES

Insulin-dependent diabetes occurs when the pancreas does not produce any insulin. Daily injections of insulin are required to regulate sugar levels.

The insulin-dependent diabetic must balance:
- Amount of insulin injected
- Exercise
- Food intake

If these are not balanced, hypoglycaemia (low blood sugar) might result.

Non insulin-dependent diabetes generally does not occur until adults are over 40 years of age. The insulin produced by the body is not being used for the conversion of glucose into energy. The glucose does not enter the cells but remains in the bloodstream. Sometimes this type of diabetes is associated with obesity.

GENERAL DIETARY RULES FOR DIABETICS

Consult and follow the doctor's recommendations.
- Follow the dietary programme recommended by the doctor for the particular type of diabetes
- Maintain the weight recommended by the doctor
- Eat snacks and meals regularly – never miss them
- Eat starchy foods evenly and regularly throughout the day and balance with insulin intake
- Reduce intake of salt and fat

Avoid:
- Sugar and sugary foods, such as pastries, cakes, biscuits, marmalades, jam, chocolate, sweets, fruits in syrup, sugary drinks

Choose:
- Wholemeal bread, rice (brown or white), pasta, potatoes, some sugar-free yoghurts

Again, check that the diabetic is allowed to include these in the diet planned for them.

Check:
- Commercial diabetic product labels
- That the product is suitable for the particular type of diabetes

OBESITY

People are considered obese when they are 20% over the recommended weight for their height.

Main causes of obesity:
- Intake of kilocalories is greater than the kilocalories used
- Hormone imbalance

Risks associated with obesity:
- Reduced life expectancy
- Heart disease
- Increased risk of high blood pressure and strokes
- Varicose veins
- Gallstones
- Diabetes
- Difficulty during pregnancy and childbirth

GENERAL DIETARY GUIDELINES
- Eat a healthy balanced varied diet (do not diet without advice from a doctor)
- Choose foods which balance energy intake with energy output
- Eat three regular meals each day (if hungry between meals choose fresh fruit or raw vegetables)
- Always eat a healthy breakfast
- Choose fruits, vegetables, lean meat, poultry, fish, low-fat dairy products, water, low-sugar foods
- Grill, bake, poach or microwave food (avoid frying)
- Increase intake of water
- Modify recipes to increase dietary fibre and reduce fat, sugar and salt
- Exercise regularly

Avoid:
- Fast foods, fried foods (chips, sausages, burgers), full-fat cheese, cream, yoghurt and milk, sugary foods and drinks, sugar in tea or coffee, cakes, biscuits

Do not shop when hungry or eat when bored or upset.

EATING DISORDERS

Some young men and women suffer from eating disorders.

Anorexia nervosa is an eating disorder which may lead to severe dieting, resulting in excessive weight loss. The body is starved of food. People suffering from this condition are convinced that they are overweight or fat, when in fact they may be well below their recommended weight.

Bulimia nervosa is different to anorexia nervosa, as those suffering from it need not be underweight. In some cases, sufferers may be a little overweight. Binge eating followed by vomiting is a symptom. People with this eating disorder sometimes take laxatives to reduce their weight.

Anorexia nervosa and Bulimia nervosa require professional attention and counselling.

3

THE DIGESTIVE SYSTEM

SOME DEFINITIONS

ABSORPTION: These small soluble molecules are absorbed into the bloodstream and distributed around the body to where they are needed.

DIGESTION: Food is broken down by the teeth and by the digestive enzymes into small soluble units or molecules.

ENZYME: An enzyme is a chemical substance that causes a reaction without changing itself.

THE SMALLEST MOLECULES

Food must be broken up into smaller pieces before it can be absorbed and used by the body. All nutrients present must be converted into their smallest molecules for absorption to take place.

THE SMALLEST MOLECULES

NUTRIENT	SMALLEST MOLECULE
Protein	Amino acid
Fat	Fatty acid and glycerol
Carbohydrate	Simple sugar, glucose
Cellulose	Cannot be broken down
Vitamins	Are already small units
Minerals	Are already small units

THE DIGESTIVE SYSTEM

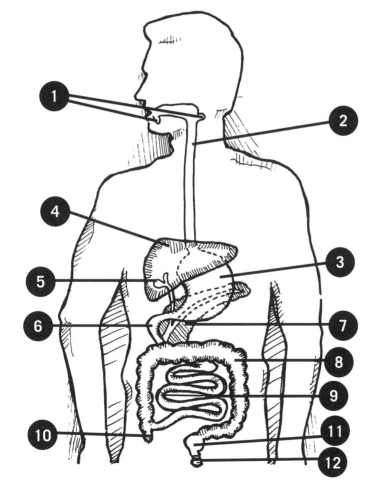

1 Salivary glands
2 Oesophagus
3 Stomach
4 Liver
5 Gall-bladder
6 Duodenum
7 Pancreas
8 Large intestine
9 Small intestine
10 Appendix
11 Rectum
12 Anus

TYPES OF DIGESTION

Physical: Food is taken into the mouth, where it is broken up and chewed by the teeth. In the stomach the food is churned. This process may also be referred to as the mechanical breakdown of food.

Chemical: During the physical process, chemicals in the form of enzymes help break down food. The enzyme causes the chemical reaction without changing itself. Different nutrients are broken down by different enzymes.

THE PATHWAY OF DIGESTION
WHAT HAPPENS TO FOOD ?

MOUTH

The teeth chop, grind, chew and break up food. The food is mixed with saliva. Saliva contains an enzyme called ptyalin. Ptyalin acts on starch, breaking it down into maltose.

Enzyme action

> **SALIVARY AMYLASE** ➜ **COOKED STARCH** ➜ **MALTOSE**

OESOPHAGUS

The mouth is linked to the stomach by the oesophagus (about 25 cm in length). Rippling, wave-like muscular movements, called peristalsis, push the food along the oesophagus into the stomach. No digestion takes place in the oesophagus.

STOMACH

The stomach is made up of muscular walls. Digestion in the stomach involves both physical and chemical processes. The food is churned around in the stomach until it forms chyme. Fats are melted by the heat of the stomach. Gastric juices, containing hydrochloric acid and the enzymes rennin and pepsin, are released from the walls of the stomach.

Enzyme action

RENNIN	➜	**MILK PROTEIN**	➜	**CURDS AND WHEY**
PEPSIN	➜	**PROTEINS**	➜	**PEPTONES**

SMALL INTESTINE

The small intestine (about 6 m in length) joins the stomach and the large intestine. Peristalsis causes the food to move along the small intestine. The pancreas releases three enzymes into the small intestine, trypsin, amylase and lipase.

Enzyme action

AMYLASE ➜ STARCH ➜ MALTOSE (SUGARS)

LIPASE ➜ FATS ➜ FATTY ACIDS AND GLYCEROL

TRYPSIN ➜ PROTEIN ➜ PEPTONES (CHAINS OF AMINO ACIDS)

The intestinal juice of the small intestine produces four enzymes, erepsin, lactase, maltase and sucrase.

Enzyme action

EREPSIN ➜ PEPTONES ➜ AMINO ACIDS

LACTASE ➜ LACTOSE ➜ GLUCOSE (SIMPLE SUGAR MOLECULE)

MALTASE ➜ MALTOSE ➜ GLUCOSE

SUCRASE ➜ SUCROSE ➜ GLUCOSE

Bile from the gall-bladder:
- Emulsifies fat, breaking it into fatty acids and glycerol
- Neutralises hydrochloric acid

LARGE INTESTINE

Here digestion is completed. The large intestine is about 2 m in length. Some vitamins B and K are produced in the large intestine. Water is reabsorbed through the walls and taken back into the body. Solid waste is removed from the rectum through the anus.

THE PATHWAY OF ABSORPTION
WHAT HAPPENS TO THE NUTRIENTS?

The inner lining of the walls of the small and large intestines contain thousands of finger-like projections called villi. The villi are made up of lacteals and blood vessels. Most absorption takes place in the small intestine. Nutrients passing into the large intestine will be absorbed through its villi.

- Fatty acids, glycerol and fat-soluble vitamins pass into the lacteals, circulate around the body and eventually enter the blood system.
- Amino acids, glucose, water-soluble vitamins and minerals are absorbed directly into the blood vessels and are transported to the rest of the body.

4

FOOD HYGIENE AND FOOD SAFETY

FOOD SPOILAGE

Foods can spoil due to micro-organisms or enzymes. Enzymes occur naturally in food.
Examples of micro-organisms: moulds, yeast and bacteria.
To avoid the growth of micro-organisms in the kitchen, food contamination and cross-contamination, it is important to keep everything clean.

FOOD POISONING

Food poisoning can result if there are high levels of bacteria present in food. Symptoms include stomach pains, nausea, vomiting and in some cases diarrhoea.

SOURCES OF FOOD POISONING

FOOD POISONING BACTERIA	SOURCES
Salmonella	Meat, sausages, shellfish, poultry
Listeria	Soft cheese, cook–chill products, pâté, poultry
Staphylococcus	Spread by humans
Clostridium	Incorrectly processed canned foods

FACTORS AFFECTING FOOD SAFETY
- Personal hygiene
- Food hygiene (food handling, preparation, cooking, serving)
- Kitchen hygiene
- Food storage

HOW BACTERIA SPREAD

Bacteria multiply and are spread in the kitchen by:
- Flies
- Vermin
- Pets in the kitchen and throughout the house
- Dirty, greasy surfaces, utensils and equipment
- Dirty kitchen cloths, towels and bins
- Cross-contamination between raw and cooked foods
- Poor personal and food hygiene
- Incorrect storage of food
- Incorrect handling of food

Conditions needed for micro-organisms to multiply:
- Food
- Warmth (around 37°C)
- Moisture (conditions and food)
- Time (bacteria double every 20 minutes)

RULES FOR PREVENTING CONTAMINATION

PERSONAL HYGIENE
- Wash hands after using the toilet
- Wash hands after handling cats, dogs, birds, etc.
- Wash hands before cooking or handling food
- Tie back hair
- Do not cough or sneeze over food and dishes
- Cover all cuts
- Do not lick your fingers when preparing and cooking food

KITCHEN HYGIENE
- Do not allow cats, dogs, etc., into the kitchen
- Keep all surfaces (kitchen units, floors, sink units, draining boards, chopping boards) clean and tidy
- Wash the kitchen floor each day
- Wash all kitchen cloths daily
- Wipe up spills as they occur

- Empty and wash the kitchen bin daily
- Keep all utensils and equipment clean
- Clean out all kitchen cupboards regularly
- Clean cooker, fridge and microwave oven frequently

FOOD HYGIENE

- Store food at the correct temperature and in the correct location in the kitchen
- Keep food covered when not in use
- Do not put cooked and raw food on the same chopping boards or dishes
- Wash hands after handling raw foods, before handling cooked foods
- Wash knives, spoons and other utensils after preparing raw meat (do not use the same equipment for raw and cooked foods without washing them)
- Cook food correctly
- Leftover food must be thoroughly reheated

Stop the multiplication of bacteria with:
- Antiseptics (reduce the level of bacteria)
- Disinfectants (kill all bacteria)

FOOD STORAGE

CLASSIFICATION OF FOODS

Foods are classified so that they may be stored correctly in the kitchen.

CLASSIFICATION OF FOODS

CLASSIFICATION	EXAMPLES	STORAGE AREA
Perishable	Milk, cream, meat, poultry, fish, eggs	Fridge
	Frozen foods	Freezer
Semi-perishable	Vegetables, fruits	Vegetable rack
Non-perishable	Tea, coffee, flour, sugar, baking ingredients, tinned foods, pasta	Kitchen cupboard

FOOD LABELLING

Food labels provide:
- A date stamp for the consumer in the form of 'sell by' date, 'best before' date or 'use before' date (check the dates on all foods that you buy)
- Storage instructions (e.g. store in a dark, dry place away from direct heat and sunlight)
- Star markings on frozen foods giving date and storage information

RULES FOR STORING FOOD

1 Store according to its class (perishable, dry)
2 Do not store food near chemicals or cleaning agents
3 Cover all foods when not being used
4 Do not mix raw and cooked foods
5 Never place hot or warm food in a fridge – allow to cool
6 Never store strong-smelling foods in a fridge (onions, etc.)
7 Store vegetables and fruit in a vegetable rack
8 Use food by the date recommended on the food label
9 Use food in rotation
10 Do not store cakes and biscuits together
11 Leftover foods should be used up quickly
12 Thawed foods must never be refrozen
13 Store opened dry foods in airtight containers
14 Clean out food cupboards and fridge regularly

FOOD STORAGE MATERIALS

- Polythene containers
- Polythene bags
- Film wrap
- Kitchen foil
- Foil containers
- Greaseproof paper
- Pyrex dishes
- Tin (biscuits and cake)

6

FOOD PROCESSING

Reasons for processing food:
- To make a wide variety of food available all year
- To make some foods more digestible
- To create new foods
- To stop the action of micro-organisms and enzymes

Examples of processed foods:
Milk, butter, cheese, yoghurt, canned foods, bottled foods, white flour, frozen meals, fruit juice, dried fruit.

Examples of new food products:
Crisps, yoghurt drinks, vegetable burgers, breakfast cereals, cook–chill meals.

CONVENIENCE FOODS

What are convenience foods?
Foods that undergo commercial preparation, pre-cooking and cooking which save cooking time and energy in the home are called convenience foods.

Advantages:
- Save time and energy
- Easy to prepare and use
- Foods can be used out of season
- Provides variety

Disadvantages:
- Expensive to use regularly
- It is easy to become dependent on them
- Some convenience foods tend to be high in salt, sugar and saturated fat and low in dietary fibre
- Incorrectly stored and cooked cook–chill products can cause food poisoning

TYPES OF CONVENIENCE FOODS

- Dried food (soups, sauces, cake mixes, bread mixes, spices, herbs, tea, coffee)
- Canned food (peas, beans, mushrooms, soups, pineapple, black cherries, salmon, tuna)
- Bottled food (jam, chutney, carrots, sauces, salad dressings, olive oil)

- Frozen food (pizza, fish, meat, vegetables, pastry, pre-cooked meals such as lasagne and garlic bread)
- Cook–chill foods (already cooked, ready for reheating)
- Take-away foods (Chinese meals, Indian meals, fish and chips)

GENERAL GUIDELINES FOR USING CONVENIENCE FOODS

1 Follow the instructions on the tin, jar or package
2 Use convenience foods in emergencies (do not use them to replace the use of fresh foods on a daily basis)
3 Combine convenience foods with fresh foods
4 Include fresh fruit and vegetables with dishes based on convenience foods to improve the nutritive value
5 Use no more than one or two convenience foods in a meal
6 Heat cook–chill products thoroughly to destroy bacteria
7 Use convenience foods in rotation

STORING CONVENIENCE FOODS

- Store canned, bottled and dry convenience foods in a dry, well-ventilated kitchen cupboard
- Store cook–chill products below 4°C

BUYING CONVENIENCE FOODS

- Buy packets, cans, jars and containers which can be recycled
- Check that packets are sealed correctly
- Do not buy bulging or damaged tins
- Choose low-salt, sugar and fat products
- Check the 'sell by' date

FOOD LABELS

European Union law states that food labels should carry specific and relevant information so that consumers are aware of what they are buying. The composition and hygiene of food is controlled by health acts and regulations and food hygiene regulations.

Information on food labels includes:
- Name of food product
- Nutritional information

- Ingredients
- Quantity
- 'Sell by', 'best before' or 'use by' date

- Cooking instructions
- Name and address of manufacturer, country of origin
- Instructions for storage

FOOD LABEL

PRODUCT A: CREAM OF TOMATO SOUP

Erin ONE PINT

Cream of Tomato Soup — A

This pack yields 570 ml (1 pint)

F — *Directions:* 1. Empty the contents of this packet into a saucepan and gradually add 190 ml (⅓ pint) milk and 380 ml (⅔ pint) cold water, stirring until blended. 2. Bring to the boil, stirring continuously; partially cover, and allow to simmer for 5 minutes, stirring occasionally.

B — *Ingredients:* Cornflour, Sugar, Dehydrated Vegetables (Tomato, Onion), Dried Milk Solids, Vegetable Fat, Salt, Milk Protein, Flavour Enhancer (621), Citric Acid, Emulsifier (E471), Yeast Extract, Colour (Apocarotenal, Annatto), Spices, Herbs. *FREE FROM ARTIFICIAL COLOURS & FLAVOURS*

NUTRITIONAL INFORMATION PER 100 ml AS SERVED	
ENERGY	308 kJ
	73 kcal
PROTEIN	2.2g
CARBOHYDRATE	10.3g
FAT	2.6g

E

Best Before:

D — 22 MAR 96 08:54:30

5 011009 008763

Approved Quality System — C

H

IRL P713 EEC

Erin Foods, Thurles, Co. Tipperary. Product of the Republic of Ireland. — G

70g ℮

A Name of food product
B Ingredients
C Quantity symbol
D 'Best before' date
E Nutritional information

F Cooking instructions
G Name and address of manufacturer, country of origin
H Bar code

....
FOOD ADDITIVES

Most convenience foods contain additives.

WHY ARE ADDITIVES USED?

Additives are used to:
- Increase the shelf-life of foods
- Improve flavour and texture
- Add nutrients to foods (fortified)
- Inhibit the action of micro-organisms and enzymes
- Prevent the food reacting to the air

Advantages of food additives:
- Improved flavour, colour and consistency
- Increased shelf-life
- Increased nutritive value (fortified)

Disadvantages of food additives:
- Allergic reactions to certain additives (e.g. tartrazine)
- Some colours look unnatural
- Foods do not follow a natural cycle until they decay

Examples of additives:
- Anti-caking agents
- Antioxidants
- Colourings
- Emulsifiers and stabilisers
- Flavourings
- Flavour enhancers
- Nutritive additives
- Preservatives
- Sweeteners

7

FOOD PRESERVATION

Reasons for preserving food:
- Destroys micro-organisms (bacteria, moulds, yeasts)
- Inhibits the action of enzymes
- Prevents micro-organisms re-entering food

- Maintains the nutritive value of the food
- Tries to keep the natural colour, flavour and texture

Advantages of preserving food:
- Prevents waste when foods are plentiful
- Provides variety in the diet when the food is out of season
- Saves time and energy, as food has been prepared
- Saves money
- Flavour of homemade preserves is excellent

Factors causing food to deteriorate:
- Action of enzymes
- Bacteria, moulds and yeasts

Micro-organisms need the following conditions to multiply:
- Air
- Moisture
- Food
- Warmth

When one or more of these conditions is removed, micro-organisms will not multiply and food will last longer.

METHODS OF PRESERVATION

CONDITION REMOVED	METHOD
Removal of air	Canning, bottling, jams
Removal of moisture	Drying
Removal of warmth	Freezing

Note: During most methods of preservation the colour, flavour and texture of the food is changed. Some methods reduce the nutritive value of the food.

FREEZING FOOD

Micro-organisms need moisture (water) to survive. All foods contain water and during freezing the water turns into ice. Micro-organisms cannot multiply or work when food is frozen. When the food thaws out, they begin to act on the food once more.

General rules for freezing:
1 Choose top quality foods
2 Turn down the freezer to the lowest temperature in preparation for the food to be frozen (turn to 'fast freeze')
3 Pack and label foods correctly

4   Freeze food in small quantities in the 'fast freeze' compartment
5   Do not pack the food tightly – allow the cold air to circulate

Remember:
Some foods need to be blanched before freezing.
Thaw frozen meat (especially poultry) completely before cooking.

Do not freeze:
Bananas, cabbage, cucumber, lettuce, melon, milk, whole eggs, whole tomatoes.

Freeze:
Bread, cakes, desserts, scones, breadcrumbs, ice-cream, meat, fish, poultry, most fruit and vegetables, uncooked pastry, pastry dishes, sauces, soups, stews and casseroles, stuffings, sweets.

Freezer packaging:
Containers must be strong and moisture-proof. They should be suitable for use at low temperatures. Examples include:

- Freezer foil containers
- Waxed cartons and tubs
- Polythene bags and boxes

JAM MAKING

When fruits are plentiful during late summer and autumn, they can be turned into jams for use out of season. High temperatures destroy the micro-organisms and by sealing the jar they cannot re-enter the food. Jars are also heated to a high temperature and are sterilised in the oven before the jam is added. Sugar acts as a preservative and jam contains a high percentage of sugar (65%).

CANNING AND BOTTLING

During the canning process, the food to be preserved is cooked and undergoes a sterilisation process in the can. Cans are air-tight. Do not purchase cans that are damaged in any way. Colour, flavour and texture change during the canning process.

CHEMICAL PRESERVATION

Chemical preservatives include:

- Acid (vinegar in pickles and chutneys)
- Smoke (smoked salmon and trout)
- Chemicals (sulphur dioxide)
- Sugar (jam, chutney)
- Salt (bacon, salted meat and fish)

DRYING FOOD (DEHYDRATION)

Moisture is removed so that micro-organisms cannot destroy the food. Water or other liquids are added in order to rehydrate the food for use. Any micro-organisms remaining in the food may become active again. Treat the food as a fresh food once it has been rehydrated.

Examples of dried foods:
- Breakfast cereals
- Fruit (raisins, sultanas)
- Packet soups, sauces, cake mixes
- Spices
- Dried milk powder
- Herbs
- Casserole mixes and gravies
- Vegetables (dried tomatoes)

OTHER METHODS

- Processing (meats)
- Vacuum packing (rashers, etc.)
- Pasteurisation (cream, milk and yoghurt)

IRRADIATION

Gamma radiation is used to preserve fruit and vegetables. This process destroys micro-organisms and insects. Strict safety standards are enforced.

8

COOKING METHODS

REASONS FOR COOKING FOOD

- Micro-organisms (bacteria, moulds, yeast) and enzymes are destroyed by heat and so food becomes safe to eat
- Food looks more appetising, colour develops (roast beef, etc.)
- Food tastes better, flavours develop (omelette)
- Cooking aromas stimulate the appetite
- Food becomes more digestible (rice, potatoes)
- Cooking preserves some foods (chutney, jam)
- Hot dishes are suitable for winter meals (beef casserole)

Some foods can be eaten raw (fruit, vegetables). These can look and taste appetising.

HEAT TRANSFER DURING COOKING

Cooking causes physical and chemical changes in the food.
Heat produced during cooking passes into the food, causing the food to cook.
Heat is transferred in three ways.

- **Conduction:** Heat passes from an area of high temperature to an area of lower temperature. It passes from one molecule to the next molecule.

    COOKER HOB ➜ FRYING PAN OR WOK ➜ FOOD

Example of cooking method: frying

- **Convection:** Gases or liquids expand and rise when heated. When they cool they become more dense and fall. Convection currents are set up which circulate heat.

    COOKER HOB ➜ SAUCEPAN WITH LIQUID ➜ FOOD
    OVEN ➜ CONVECTION AIR CURRENTS ➜ FOOD

Examples of cooking method: boiling, stewing, roasting

- **Radiation:** Heat travels in straight lines in the form of rays.

    GRILL ➜ HEAT RAYS ➜ FOOD

Examples of cooking method: grilling, toasting, barbecuing

METHODS OF COOKING	
METHODS	**EXAMPLES**
Dry heat	Grilling or barbecuing
	Baking
Moist heat	Poaching
	Simmering
	Boiling
	Stewing
	Braising
	Steaming
Using fat	Roasting
	Frying (shallow or deep-fat)
Microwave	

DRY HEAT

GRILLING

Grilling uses intense radiant heat at high temperatures to cook food in a short time under the cooker grill or on the barbecue.

Foods to choose:
Rashers, sausages, burgers, steak, kidneys, chops, cutlets, fish, au gratin dishes, tomatoes, mushrooms, small thin pieces of vegetables, toast, sandwiches.

Cooking times:
Fillet steak	6–15 mins (rare to well done)
Lamb chops	8–12 mins
Rashers	4–5 mins
Kidney	5–6 mins

Cooking guidelines for grilling:
1 Choose food which can be cooked quickly.
2 Season food with pepper and avoid salt, which draws out the juices.
3 Always pre-heat the grill before cooking.
4 Brush grill grid with oil to prevent food sticking.
5 Brush food with melted fat or oil to prevent burning or drying out.
6 Seal both sides of the food quickly, so that juices do not escape.
7 Turn food frequently using tongs (do not use a fork).

BAKING

Baking uses dry radiant heat in an oven to cook food. Heat is transferred by convection. Baked foods have a crisp outer surface.

Foods to choose:
Bread, pastries, cakes, biscuits, pies (sweet and savoury), puddings, fish, vegetables, potatoes, fruit.

Cooking guidelines for baking:
1 Pre-heat the oven to the correct temperature (this is important when baking breads and cakes which contain a raising agent).
2 Do not overfill the oven. Allow space for air currents to circulate.
3 Avoid using the oven just for one dish. When baking, make

maximum use of the oven. This saves energy and is economical.

4   Avoid opening the oven door frequently.

5   To keep some foods moist, use foil during the cooking process. Remove before cooking is completed to crisp up the surface.

6   Use oven gloves when removing the hot dishes from the oven.

MOIST HEAT

POACHING

Poaching means cooking food in gently moving liquid between 85°C and 90°C in an open saucepan or poaching pan. Cooking is by conduction. Poaching is not a fast method of cooking, but it is not as slow as boiling or stewing. Poaching can be carried out on a hob or in an oven.

Foods to choose:
Eggs, fish, fruit.

Cooking guidelines for poaching:
1   Read the recipe carefully. Some foods need to be poached starting with cold liquid, others can be put into warm liquid.

2   Choose a suitable saucepan (shallow or deep).

3   Suitable poaching liquids include water, stock, milk, syrup, fruit juice and wine.

4   Barely cover the food with liquid.

5   Do not leave the saucepan unattended, as the food can overcook and fall apart.

6   Remove poached foods using a slotted spoon or a fish slice.

7   Drain food on kitchen paper.

BOILING

Boiling means cooking food in a fast-moving liquid at 100°C in an open or covered saucepan. Heat is transferred by conduction.

Foods to choose:
Vegetables, fresh meat, salted meat, fish, eggs, cereals, rice, pasta.

Others: Boiling is also used when making sauce, jam, chutney, marmalade, stock and syrup.

Cooking guidelines for boiling:
1 Choose a suitable saucepan with a well-fitted lid.
2 Some foods need to be put into fast boiling water (green leafy vegetables). Do not overcook vegetables. Other foods are put into cold water and then brought to the boil (salted meat).
3 Barely cover the food with liquid. Use the minimum of liquid when cooking vegetables.
4 Add herbs, seasoning, vegetables and stock to develop flavours.
5 Watch carefully, as food can fall apart if allowed to boil for too long. Reduce heat slightly to prevent this happening.
6 Use all leftover cooking liquid for sauces, stocks and soups, as it contains minerals and water-soluble vitamins.
7 Remove the food using a slotted spoon and drain.

STEWING AND CASSEROLING

Stewing is a long, slow method of cooking even-sized pieces of food in liquid in a saucepan with a well-fitting lid. It can be done on the hob or in the oven (casseroling). Stewing tenderises tough foods and is an economical method of cooking. The cooking liquid is generally served as part of the dish.

Foods to choose:
Tough, cheap cuts of meat (neck, shin or rib beef, mutton), poultry, fish, root and pulse vegetables, fruit.

Cooking guidelines for stewing:
1 Remove excess fat from meat and poultry.
2 All food should be cut into even-sized pieces.
3 Bring the liquid to boiling point and reduce the temperature.
4 Barely cover the food with liquid. Cook slowly.
5 Cover the saucepan or dish with a tightly fitting lid.
6 Check from time to time.
7 Use oven gloves to remove casserole dish from the oven.

STEAMING

Steaming is a slow method of cooking food over steam rising from a saucepan of boiling water on the hob. The food may or may not come into contact with the steam. The liquid does not come into contact with the food. Steaming can be done using two plates over a saucepan, a steamer, bamboo baskets, a pressure cooker, or in a pudding bowl.

Foods to choose:
Thin pieces of meat, poultry and fish, savoury and sweet puddings, egg custards, potatoes, root vegetables, new vegetables, rice.

Cooking guidelines for steaming:
1   Rapidly boiling water is essential.
2   Bring the water to boiling point before cooking begins.
3   Never allow the water and the food to come into contact with each other.
4   Pay attention if using a pressure cooker for steaming. Follow the manufacturer's instructions.
5   Never allow the saucepan to boil dry.
6   Season foods to make up for the lack of flavour.

USING HOT FAT

ROASTING

Roasting is a method of cooking food in a small amount of hot fat at high temperatures, in an oven or on a rotating spit. Food is placed on a roasting tin, rotisserie, casserole dish or in roasting bags.

Foods to choose:
Joints of meat, poultry, game (pheasant, rabbit, duck, venison), potatoes, root vegetables, nuts.

Cooking guidelines for roasting:
1   Pre-heat the oven to the recommended temperature.
2   Do not place food directly from the fridge into the oven. Allow food to reach room temperature.
3   Prepare food and calculate the cooking time.
4   Baste food with hot fat and continue to baste during the cooking.
5   If the meat is tender, quick roast it. If tough, slow roast it.
6   Remove roasting dish from the oven using oven gloves.
7   Allow to stand and drain for 10 minutes. Carve and serve.

FRYING

Frying is a quick method of cooking food in hot fat or oil. Extra fat is absorbed by the food during frying, as the food is directly in contact with the fat or oil. Heat is conducted from the hob through the frying pan to the food.

Nutritionally, frying is not the best method of cooking and frying should be avoided as a method of cooking where possible.

Methods of frying:

Deep-fat frying	Food is immersed in hot oil or fat in a saucepan or a deep-fat fryer.
Dry frying	Food is cooked in a shallow pan without fat or oil.
Shallow frying	Thin pieces of food are fried in a small amount of fat or oil in a shallow pan.
Stir-frying	Small pieces of food are cooked very quickly in hot oil in a wok.

Foods to choose:

Thin, tender pieces of meat, offal, poultry, fish, vegetables, rashers, sausages, potato chips, doughnuts, fritters, rissoles, burgers, coated foods (fish).

Cooking guidelines for frying:

1 Never leave frying pans, deep-fat fryers or woks unattended.
2 Prepare the food before heating the oil or fat.
3 Dry food with kitchen paper to remove moisture.
4 Never allow water and hot oil to come into contact with each other.
5 Pre-heat the oil or fat before adding the food.
6 Use clean oil. Choose polyunsaturated oils rather than saturated fats.
7 Be careful as you place the food into the hot oil.
8 Seal both sides of the food to keep in the juices.
9 Remove cooked food carefully with a slotted spoon, drain and keep warm.
10 Turn off cooker switches and unplug deep-fat fryers as soon as cooking is completed.
11 Allow oil to cool, strain and put into suitable containers.

MEAL PLANNING

Meal planning is influenced by:
- Time available
- Time of year or season
- Fresh foods available
- The occasion
- Money available
- Number of people
- Skills of the cook
- Equipment available
- Special dietary needs or restrictions
- Individual tastes or preferences
- Lifestyle

Choice of individual dishes is influenced by:
- All the above points
- Balance of colours, flavours and textures
- Variety of ingredients and dishes
- Presentation and garnishes

GUIDELINES FOR MEAL PLANNING

- Plan ahead – make a shopping list based on the menus for one week
- Choose foods in season (cheaper than out-of-season foods)
- Avoid repetition
- Plan to use all leftovers
- Serve hot dishes in winter and chilled dishes in summer
- Vary cooking methods
- If time is limited, choose fast methods of cooking
- Use equipment that will speed up the preparation and cooking time
- Keep in mind the latest nutritional guidelines
- Plan accompaniments, garnishes and decorations to suit the dishes being served

MENUS

SOME DEFINITIONS

MENU: A menu is an organised list of all the dishes to be served during a meal.

TABLE D'HÔTE MENU: This is a restaurant menu which has a fixed price for the complete meal. Three to five courses may be offered, with limited choices for each course. It is cheaper than the à la carte restaurant menu.

À LA CARTE MENU: This menu lists every dish possible for all courses, with individual prices beside each dish. It offers more choice than the table d'hôte menu. A complete meal based on this type of menu generally works out more expensive.

WRITING MENU CARDS

- Create an attractive design
- Write courses in the order they will be eaten
- Write names of dishes down the centre of the menu card
- Describe the dish correctly; name the type of meat and state how it will be cooked
- List the accompaniments (vegetables, sauces)

SAMPLE MENU

Chilled kiwi salad

★★★★★

Roast leg of lamb
Mint sauce
Creamed potatoes
Buttered carrots

★★★★★

Home-made chocolate ice-cream

GUIDELINES FOR SETTING THE TABLE

- Table linen, delph, glasses and cutlery should be spotlessly clean
- Arrange cutlery in the order in which it will be used
- Allow sufficient space for each person
- Fill all condiment sets and arrange in groups on the table
- Organise an attractive floral, fresh fruit or candle centrepiece for the table

GUIDELINES FOR PRESENTING AND SERVING FOOD

- Food should look attractive
- Food should be arranged neatly on clean plates or dishes

- Serve cold or chilled food on cold plates
- Serve hot food piping hot on warmed plates
- Use plain plates and dishes for serving savoury foods
- Choose fancy plates and dishes for sweet foods
- Serve meat towards the centre of the plate
- Serve sauces in a sauce-boat or on the plate around the meat
- Garnish savoury dishes, decorate sweet dishes (garnish and decorate food lightly)

GARNISHES

Croûtons
Finely chopped parsley
Sprigs of parsley
Lemon twists or slices
Orange twists or slices
Twists of cucumber
Sprigs of mint
Juliennes of vegetables
Radishes
Chopped chives
Cream or yoghurt

DECORATIONS

Cherries
Piped cream
Grated chocolate
Chocolate leaves
Melted chocolate
Almond flakes

10

SAMPLE DISHES FOR BREAKFAST, LUNCH, DINNER AND TEATIME

Menus for breakfast, lunch, dinner and a light evening meal can be created by selecting from the dishes below.

BREAKFAST

Fruit: Grapefruit (segments or grilled half), melon, mixed fresh fruit salad, stewed prunes, apples.

Cereals:	Breakfast cereals (Weetabix, porridge, muesli).
Breads:	Wholemeal brown bread, toast, croissants, scones.
Cooked dishes:	Eggs (boiled, scrambled, poached), rashers, sausages, white and black pudding, liver, grilled tomato and mushroom, fish (kippers, trout), kedgeree.
Others:	Yoghurt, cheese, marmalade, jam.
Beverages:	Juice (orange, grapefruit, apple, pineapple), tea, coffee, milk.

LIGHT LUNCH

Soup:	Potato and leek, carrot, mixed vegetable, gazpacho, French onion.
Breads:	Wholemeal brown bread, bread rolls, garlic bread.
Sandwiches:	Salad, meat (beef, turkey, ham), cheese, mixed.

Main dishes:
- Baked potato with filling (chicken, ham, mushroom), green salad, coleslaw
- Pizza, green salad, coleslaw
- Lasagne, mixed green salad

Desserts:
- Fresh whole fruit (apple, pear, orange)
- Yoghurt (natural, fruit flavoured, whole fruit)

SUBSTANTIAL LUNCH

Soup:	Tomato, mushroom, minestrone, chicken broth.
Breads:	Wholemeal brown rolls and bread, dinner buns, melba toast.

Main course:
- Pasta dishes (lasagne, spaghetti bolognaise, salad)
- Salads (ham, beef, chicken, turkey, tuna)
- Quiche with salad
- Omelette with salad and baked potato

- Stuffed peppers, mixed salads
- Kebabs, green salad
- Grilled chicken, green salad, brown rice salad
- Grilled trout, green salad, brown rice salad
- Savoury stuffed pancakes, mixed salad

Desserts:
- Yoghurt with stewed fruit
- Fresh fruit salad
- Fruit flan
- Piece of fresh fruit (orange, pear)

MAIN MEAL (DINNER)

Starters:
- Smoked fish pâté, brown bread
- Salad Niçoise
- Mixed fruit salad
- Melon balls
- Seafood cocktail
- Canapés

Soups:
Any soup (broths, clear, purée, thickened) or chowders served with garlic bread, brown bread, dinner rolls or buns

Main course dishes and accompaniments:
- Baked stuffed fish (cod, trout), garden peas, creamed potatoes
- Grilled mackerel, chipped potatoes, french beans
- Goujons of fish, chipped potatoes, garden peas
- Smoked haddock au gratin, creamed potatoes, broccoli

- Stir-fry (meat, poultry, vegetables), Chinese noodles, salad
- Chilli con carne, boiled rice, green salad
- Lasagne, mixed green salad, coleslaw
- Curry (beef or chicken), boiled brown rice, green salad
- Chicken risotto, mixed salad

- Beef casserole, baked potato, french beans
- Beef goulash, piped potatoes, green salad
- Grilled steak, baked potato, mixed green salad
- Irish stew, root vegetables
- Steak and kidney pie, baked potato, green salad

- Chicken marengo, baked potato, green salad
- Roast chicken, roast potatoes, glazed carrots

- Boiled bacon and cabbage, boiled potatoes, onion sauce
- Stuffed pork steak, baked potato, mixed green salad

- Vegetarian lasagne, mixed green salad, nut salad
- Vegetarian curry, brown rice, cooked green vegetables
- Vegetarian casserole, stir-fry peppers and nuts
- Vegetable stir-fry, boiled brown rice, green salad

Desserts:
- Fresh fruit salad
- Baked apples, custard sauce
- Apple or rhubarb crumble, custard sauce
- Stewed fruit, yoghurt
- Yoghurt
- Chocolate mousse
- Cheesecake (lemon, strawberry, raspberry)
- Queen of puddings
- Stuffed pancakes
- Lemon mousse
- Strawberries and cream

LIGHT EVENING MEAL (TEATIME)

Savoury dishes:
- Cold meat or poultry salad
- Macaroni cheese, mixed salad
- Potato and cheese pie
- Eggs (omelette, boiled, poached, scrambled)
- Stuffed eggs, tomato salad
- Stuffed savoury pancakes, green salad
- Stuffed tomatoes, wholemeal bread
- Shepherd's pie, green salad, tomato salad
- Selection of sandwiches

Bread and cakes:
- Wholemeal brown bread
- Brown fruit scones
- Fruit flan
- Apple tart
- Swiss roll
- Light fruitcake
- Victoria sandwich
- Rock buns
- Tea scones
- Gingerbread

Beverages: Tea, coffee, milk.

Select garnishes, decorations, accompaniments, including sauces, to suit the dish.

11

THE CEREALS, BREAD AND POTATO FOOD GROUP

<u>LATEST NUTRITIONAL GUIDELINES</u>

Choose six servings from this food group each day. They are in the 'eat most' food group.

CEREALS

Cereals consist of wheat, oats, barley, rye, corn and rice. The cereal group is made up also of the products associated with them (bread, cakes, pastry, pasta, sandwiches).

<u>NUTRITIVE VALUE</u>

Protein:	Vegetable proteins in small amounts (gluten is a protein found in cereals)
Fat:	Traces in the germ
Carbohydrate:	Starch (75%) in the endosperm and cellulose in the bran
Vitamins:	B-group vitamins
Minerals:	Calcium, iron and phosphorus
Water:	Low water content

Cereals are available in many forms. Wholegrain cereals and their products provide dietary fibre and B-group vitamins. When cereals are refined, they lose both fibre and vitamin B, and a high percentage of starch remains. Because of the loss of nutrients during processing, some cereals are fortified. Cereals contain LBV protein. Coeliacs must not use wheat because it contains gluten (they cannot break down gluten).

<u>WHEAT</u>

The wheat grain is made up of three sections: the outer bran layer, the inside layer (endosperm) and the germ.
The bran provides dietary fibre and iron.
The endosperm consists mainly of gluten and starch.
The germ contains dietary fibre, protein, traces of fat and B-group vitamins.

WHEAT GRAIN

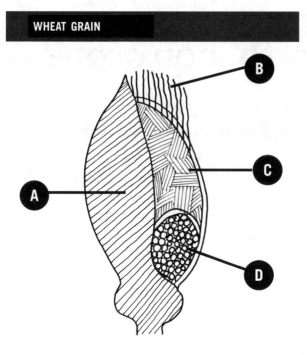

A Outer bran or husk
B Beard
C Endosperm
D Germ

The bran and germ are removed during the milling process.

TYPES OF FLOUR IN THE SHOPS

- **Wholemeal flour:** 100% extraction rate (nothing removed)
- **Wheaten meal or brown flour:** 80–90% extraction rate (some bran is removed)
- **White flour:** Approx 70% extraction rate (all the bran and most of the germ is removed)
- **Strong plain flour:** High gluten content flour
- **Self-raising flour:** White flour with added raising agent
- **Gluten-free flour:** For use in coeliac diets

White flour is fortified or enriched with calcium, iron and B-group vitamins.

EXAMPLES OF REFINED CEREAL PRODUCTS

White flour	White rice	Cornflour
White bread	White scones	Pastry
Rice flakes		

EXAMPLES OF CEREAL PRODUCTS

PRODUCT	CEREAL
Cornflakes	Corn/maize
Porridge	Oats
Rice krispies	Rice
Pasta	Wheat

BREADS AND CAKES

Breads and cakes are made using flour, fat, sugar, a raising agent and liquid (water or eggs or milk).

RAISING AGENTS

Raising agents are added to bread and cakes to raise the mixture.
A gas is produced which expands when heated, raising the bread or cake.
A crust forms to prevent the mixture from rising further.

Types of raising agents:

NATURAL – Air (added when sieving flour, rubbing in fat, creaming fat and sugar, whisking eggs)

CHEMICAL – Baking powder; Bread soda and sour milk

ACID + ALKALI + LIQUID = CARBON DIOXIDE

BIOLOGICAL – Yeast

BASIC METHODS FOR MAKING CAKES

- **Rubbing-in:** Fat into flour (scones, pastry, plain cakes)
- **Creaming:** Fat into sugar (rich fruitcake, Madeira buns)
- **Whisking:** Sugar and eggs (swiss roll, egg sponge)
- **Melted fat:** Melt fat, add to dry ingredients (gingerbread)
- **All-in-one:** Madeira cakes, pastry (using soft margarine)

EXAMPLES OF RAISING AGENTS IN ACTION

BREADS/CAKES	RAISING AGENT
Wholemeal bread	Bread soda + sour milk
Madeira cake	Baking powder, air
Tea scones	Baking powder, air
Egg sponge	Air
Victoria sandwich	Baking powder, air
Barm brack	Yeast
Croissants	Yeast

PASTRY

Pastry is made from a mixture of fat and flour which is usually held together with a small amount of water. Pastry is suitable for sweet and savoury dishes. The raising agent used is air.

CLASSIFICATION AND USES OF PASTRY

PASTRY	USES
Shortcrust	Apple tarts, chicken pie, fruit flans
Rich shortcrust	Tarts, pies
Wholemeal	Rhubarb tart, pie, quiche
Cheese	Cheese straws, quiche, cheese biscuits
Flaky and rough puff	Sausage rolls, fish pies and sweet pies, tarts and flans
Puff	Mince pies, vol-au-vents
Choux	Eclairs, profiteroles
Filo	Fish pie, fruit parcels
Suet	Steamed or baked puddings

GENERAL GUIDELINES FOR PASTRY MAKING

1   Weigh and measure ingredients (fat, flour, water) accurately
2   Keep utensils and ingredients cold
3   Preheat the oven
4   Handle the ingredients lightly. Lift your fingers above the ingredients to introduce as much air as possible
5   Add the water gradually; avoid adding it all at once
6   Use a knife to mix in the water
7   Sprinkle flour on a clean surface

8 Knead lightly with the tips of the fingers

9 Roll out the pastry evenly without stretching it

10 Put it on a clean plate, cover and leave to rest in the fridge for 15 minutes

11 Make up dish and decorate

12 Cook pastry in a preheated hot oven

RICE

Brown rice: The husk has been removed

White rice: The bran and germ have been removed

Processed rice: Has been treated so that it cooks quickly

TYPES AND USES OF RICE

TYPES	USES
Brown rice	Brown rice salad, casseroles
Long grain pork	Kedgeree, savoury dishes, sweet and sour
Medium grain	Rice and red pepper salad, savoury dishes e.g. risotto
Short grain	Milk pudding, paella

Rice is also available as a 'cook-in-the-bag' product for faster cooking. Rice can be:

- Boiled
- Braised or baked
- Fried

Quantities per person: 50 g approx.

RICE PRODUCTS

Rice products available include rice cakes, rice flour, breakfast cereals and tinned rice pudding.

EFFECTS OF COOKING

- Rice grains soften and swell
- Starch absorbs moisture and gelatinises

PASTA

Originating in Italy, pasta is available in a variety of shapes and sizes. Pasta is made from durum wheat which has a high gluten content. Pasta can be bought fresh or dried. It comes in different colours, depending on the ingredients. Pasta should be cooked until it is 'al dente'.

PASTA SHAPES

Spaghetti, macaroni, noodles, cannelloni, ravioli, vermicelli, stars, spirals, shells.

TYPES OF PASTA

Pasta comes in a variety of colours based on the ingredients used.

- **White pasta:** plain pasta with nothing added
- **Red pasta:** with tomato
- **Pasta verde or green pasta:** with spinach
- **Pasta tricolore:** with tomato, spinach and egg
- **Brown pasta:** made with wholemeal flour

USES OF PASTA

- Pasta salads (tuna and pasta shell salad)
- As part of a main course (cannelloni)
- As a main course, with a sauce (macaroni cheese, spaghetti bolognaise)
- As an alternative to potatoes or rice
- As an accompaniment (buffet meal, Italian menu)

EFFECTS OF COOKING

The pasta softens, absorbs water and swells.

POTATOES

Potatoes are the only vegetable belonging to this food group. They are separate from the Fruit and Vegetable food group. In Ireland they are a staple food.

VALUE IN THE DIET

Potatoes provide us with vegetable protein, dietary fibre, starch, some iron, calcium, phosphorus and sodium, vitamin C and B-group vitamins. Potatoes contain no fat. Their fat content is determined by the other ingredients served with them (butter, etc.)

USES OF POTATOES

- As a snack (filled baked potato)
- As an accompaniment
- As an ingredient for savoury scones
- In soups and stews
- Reheated (potato cakes)
- As a garnish (piped potatoes)

Potatoes can be:
- Boiled
- Baked
- Creamed
- Chipped
- Roasted

Potatoes are used in convenience soups, sauces and cook–chill products and to make a variety of crisps.

12

THE FRUIT AND VEGETABLE FOOD GROUP

LATEST NUTRITIONAL GUIDELINES

Choose four servings from this food group each day.
Fruit and vegetables are essential for a balanced diet.

FRUIT

NUTRITIVE VALUE

Protein: Most fruits have a trace of protein
Fat: None, except for avocados and olives
Carbohydrate: Most fruits have sugars and starch; the outer skin contains dietary fibre or cellulose

Vitamins: Rich supply of vitamin A and C; vitamin E is also present
Minerals: Good supply of calcium and iron
Water: Very high content – fresh fruit 80–90%, dried fruit 15–20%

Fruit is available fresh, canned, bottled, frozen and in other food products. Fruit provides a good source of vitamins A and C and of minerals. It is one of our main supplies of vitamin C.

Fruit, especially if eaten with the skin, provides an excellent supply of dietary fibre in the diet. Fresh fruit has a high water content. In dried fruit the water content is reduced. Choose fruit as a snack food between meals.

USES OF FRUIT

- For breakfast (on its own, with yoghurt, on cereals)
- As a starter or first course of a meal
- As a snack between meals
- In bread, cakes, tarts, biscuits, pies
- In desserts (flans, tarts, puddings, mousse, soufflé)
- As an accompaniment to a main dish (stewed apple with pork)
- In jam and chutney
- In beverages (milk shakes, fruit juices)

CLASSIFICATION OF FRUIT

CLASS	EXAMPLE
Citrus	Oranges, lemons, limes, grapefruits
Hard	Apples, pears
Berry	Strawberry, blackberry, gooseberry
Stone	Peach, plum, cherries
Dried	Raisins, prunes, sultanas, currants, figs
Tropical	Fig, mango, papaya, star fruit
Others	Rhubarb, bananas, melon

GRADING OF FRUIT

GRADE	QUALITY
Class extra	Best quality and most expensive
Class I	Good quality
Class II	Variation in shape, colour and skin
Class III	Inferior but marketable and cheaper

GENERAL GUIDELINES FOR BUYING FRESH FRUIT

1 Buy in season
2 Check the grade of fruit
3 Buy loose whenever possible
4 Buy fruit that is just ripe
5 Use quickly; do not leave around for more than a few days

RULES FOR USING FRUIT

1 Eat raw and unpeeled when possible
2 Prepare just before serving
3 Wash thoroughly
4 Remove skin or peel only if necessary
5 Remove stones and section fruit
6 Use immediately
7 Toss bananas and apples in lemon juice to prevent oxidation

EFFECTS OF COOKING ON FRUIT

- Some fruits become more digestible
- Cooking destroys micro-organisms, enzymes and most vitamin C
- The texture of fruit is changed
- Minerals escape into cooking liquids

Fruit can be:
- Stewed
- Poached
- Baked
- Grilled
- Fried

VEGETABLES

NUTRITIVE VALUE

Protein: Good supplies of vegetable protein are found in pulse vegetables (peas, beans and lentils)

Fat: A few vegetables contain a little, but most are deficient in fat

Carbohydrate: Good supply of starch in potatoes, pulses and root vegetables; cellulose is found in all vegetables; beetroot, tomatoes and carrots provide a good supply of sugar

Vitamins: Vegetables are important for their vitamin A and C content; pulse vegetables contain vitamin B
Minerals: Important source of calcium, iron, phosphorus
Water: A large amount, varying from 75–95% in fresh vegetables

Vegetables are an important source of dietary fibre, vitamins and minerals in the diet. Green vegetables are an excellent source of calcium and iron. Pulse vegetables are a good source of vegetable protein, making them important in vegetarian diets.

Vegetables are suitable for low-fat diets because of their low fat content. They provide dietary fibre, which adds bulk to the diet. Vegetables contain vitamin E and the anti-oxidant vitamins A and C. Vegetables are available fresh, frozen, canned and bottled.

USES OF VEGETABLES

- As a starter of a meal (salmon salad, etc.)
- In soup (mixed vegetable soup, etc.)
- As a snack between meals (carrot or celery sticks)
- In savoury bread, tarts, pies (onion bread, quiche)
- As an accompaniment to a main dish (buttered carrots, etc.)
- As a main dish (vegetable curry, vegetable casserole)
- In chutney (tomato and onion chutney)
- Juices (carrot juice, tomato juice)

CLASSIFICATION OF VEGETABLES

GREENS	ROOTS	PULSES	FRUITS
Cabbage	Parsnip	Peas	Pepper
Broccoli	Carrot	Beans	Tomato
Spinach	Turnip	Lentils	Courgette
Kale	Potato		Cucumber
Cauliflower	Onion		Avocado

Others: Fennel, chicory, squash, artichoke, okra, aubergine, sweet potato, endive.

GRADING OF VEGETABLES

The grading of vegetables is the same as for fruit: Class extra, Class I, Class II and Class III.

GENERAL GUIDELINES FOR BUYING FRESH VEGETABLES

1 Buy vegetables when in season
2 Buy in small quantities and check the grade or class
3 Choose fresh and clean vegetables; avoid vegetables that are wilted and soft with blemishes
4 Choose medium-sized vegetables that have an unbroken skin and even colour
5 Check the 'best before' date

RULES FOR STORING VEGETABLES

1 Pulses are best stored in an air-tight jar
2 Salad vegetables and greens are best put into the vegetable drawer in the lower part of the fridge
3 Store roots and tubers in a cool, well-ventilated vegetable rack in a dark, dry place
4 Always remove vegetables from plastic bags and packaging
5 Store frozen vegetables in the freezer

RULES FOR USING VEGETABLES

1 Use vegetables in rotation and prepare near to serving time
2 Eat raw where possible
3 Prepare just before serving; trim sparingly
4 Wash under running water; avoid steeping and soaking; scrub roots and tubers well; remove wilted outer leaves
5 Do not mix washed and unwashed vegetables
6 Use a sharp knife when preparing vegetables to prevent loss of vitamin C
7 Cook frozen vegetables directly from the freezer

EFFECTS OF COOKING ON VEGETABLES

- Starch cells burst and vegetables become more digestible
- Cooking destroys micro-organisms and enzymes
- Vitamins and minerals are dissolved into the cooking liquid
- Most vitamin C is lost
- Cellulose or dietary fibre is softened as vegetables absorb water and swell
- Cooking changes the flavour, colour and texture
- Overcooking causes vegetables to break up

Vegetables can be:
- Boiled
- Stir-fried
- Steamed
- Braised
- Fried
- Grilled
- Microwaved
- Baked

WAYS OF RETAINING MAXIMUM VITAMIN AND MINERAL CONTENT

- Choose fresh fruit and vegetables when possible
- Buy in small quantities
- Eat raw, unpeeled if possible, but wash or scrub before eating
- Avoid steeping in water; wash under running water
- Use a sharp knife to avoid damaging the cells
- Cook in a small amount of rapidly boiling liquid for a short time in a saucepan with a well-fitting lid
- When cooking greens (e.g. cabbage) do not use bread soda
- Serve immediately with freshly chopped parsley or other herbs, tossed in butter or with a sauce
- Use the cooking liquid in sauces, stocks and soups

13

THE MILK, CHEESE AND YOGHURT GROUP

LATEST NUTRITIONAL GUIDELINES

Choose three servings from this food group daily.

MILK AND MILK PRODUCTS

VALUE IN THE DIET

Milk is an excellent source of HBV protein. Whole milk provides calcium and phosphorus, together with vitamin D for developing healthy bones and teeth.

Vitamins A and B are also present in whole milk. Some low-fat milk and whole milk is fortified with extra calcium and vitamins. Milk has a high water content. Milk is the perfect food for the first six months of a baby's life.

TYPES OF MILK

- Condensed milk
- Dried or powdered milk
- Evaporated milk
- Pasteurised whole milk
- Homogenised milk
- Ultra-heat-treatment (UHT)

Others: Skimmed, low-fat, soya milk (from soya beans).

USES OF MILK IN THE DIET

- To enrich other foods or dishes
- On its own or as part of a beverage (milk shakes)
- Over breakfast cereals
- As part of a dish (macaroni cheese, etc.)
- In sauces (parsley sauce, etc.)
- In puddings (rice pudding, etc.)
- In desserts (stuffed pancakes, etc.)

GENERAL GUIDELINES FOR STORING MILK

1 If milk is delivered to the house, remove it from direct sunlight immediately
2 Store in the fridge
3 Keep away from strong-smelling foods
4 Cover the container when not in use
5 Use milk in rotation and do not mix fresh and stale milk
6 Check the 'use by' date

EFFECTS OF COOKING ON MILK

- Protein coagulates and a skin forms on the surface
- Changes occur in the flavour
- Some vitamin B and C is lost
- Bacteria are killed when milk is boiled

Milk products:
- Cream
- Butter
- Yoghurt
- Cheese

CREAM

Cream is made from milk fat. It contains fat and the fat-soluble vitamins A and D.

TYPES OF CREAM

Fresh cream:
- Single cream
- Double cream
- Soured cream
- Low-fat cream

Convenience cream:
- UHT cream
- Tinned cream

USES OF CREAM

- Decoration of sweet dishes (piped, etc.)
- Filling for sponges (jam and cream sponge, etc.)
- Garnish for soup (blob of cream)
- Desserts (mousse, soufflé, ice cream)
- Decoration for fresh fruit salads
- In sauces
- In stews
- In salad dressings

BUTTER

Butter is made from cream. Buttermilk is the liquid left behind.

TYPES OF BUTTER

- Cream butter
- Spreadable butter
- Low-fat spreadable butter
- Unsalted butter

USES OF BUTTER

- As a spread
- In sauces
- In butter fillings for cakes
- In cake making
- With potatoes
- For sautéing vegetables, meat, etc.

YOGHURT

Yoghurt is a convenience food made from milk which has been thickened by bacteria. Full-fat and low-fat varieties are available. Yoghurt can be plain or flavoured.

TYPES OF YOGHURT

- Natural yoghurt
- Low-fat yoghurt
- Fruit yoghurt
  (flavoured or full fruit)
- Greek yoghurt
- Frozen yoghurt
- Set yoghurt
- Yoghurt drinks

USES OF YOGHURT

- As a snack
- Instead of a dessert
- As part of a packed lunch
- As a drink (in milk shakes, etc.)
- As a salad dressing
- As a savoury dip
- Instead of cream
- In stews, casseroles, sauces

CHEESE

Cheese may be made from the milk of cows, goats, sheep and some other animals.

VALUE IN THE DIET

Cheese is rich in HBV protein, vitamins A and B and calcium. The calcium and phosphorus content makes it a good food for children and pregnant women. Cheese is high in saturated fat and should be used cautiously by those with high cholesterol problems. It lacks carbohydrate. Serve with carbohydrate-rich foods. Cheese is an alternative to meat, poultry and fish in the diet. Water content varies with the type of cheese.

MAKING CHEESE

1 Milk is pasteurised
2 Rennet, an enzyme, is added to the milk
3 The mixture separates into curds and whey
4 The whey is removed
5 After draining, chopping and salting, the curd is pressed into moulds and left to mature

CLASSIFICATION OF CHEESE

TYPES	EXAMPLES
Hard	Cheddar, Kilmeaden
Semi-soft cheese	Edam, Port Salut
Soft cheese	Cottage, Brie
Blue-veined	Cashel Blue, Stilton
Processed	Galtee
Irish farmhouse	Coolea, Milleens

GENERAL GUIDELINES FOR STORING CHEESE

1 Check the 'best before' label
2 Buy in small quantities
3 Remove plastic wrapping (except for 'Easy Singles')
4 Store in the fridge, loosely wrapped in greaseproof paper
5 Remove from the fridge one hour before using to allow the flavour to develop

USES OF CHEESE

- In sauces (cheese mornay, etc.)
- As a snack on its own
- In salads
- As a garnish (grated cheese)
- As an accompaniment (sliced with cold meat salad)
- As part of a main course (quiche, macaroni cheese)
- As part of a dessert (cheesecake)
- To finish a meal as a separate course (cheeseboard)

IMPROVING THE DIGESTIBILITY OF CHEESE

This can be done by:
- Grating cheese
- Using mustard
- Combining cheese with starchy foods (bread, pasta, etc.)
- Using cheese raw rather than cooked

EFFECTS OF COOKING ON CHEESE

- Fat in cheese melts
- Overcooking makes cheese indigestible and stringy
- Cheese browns if grilled or baked
- Protein coagulates

14

MEAT, FISH AND ALTERNATIVES

LATEST NUTRITIONAL GUIDELINES

Choose two servings from this food group daily.

MEAT

SOURCES OF MEAT

Cattle: Beef, veal
Sheep: Lamb, mutton
Pig: Pork, bacon, ham
Poultry: Turkey, chicken, duck
Game: Rabbit, pheasant, duck, venison

NUTRITIVE VALUE

Protein:	Good source of HBV protein
Carbohydrate:	None present
Fat:	All meat contains saturated fat (visible and invisible fat). Beef and pork contain more fat than chicken
Minerals:	Calcium, iron and phosphorus
Vitamins:	B-group vitamins
Water:	Reasonably high water content

Meat is a rich source of high biological value protein. It is recommended that we choose lean cuts of red meat to reduce our intake of saturated fat and to reduce our consumption of red meat. It can be replaced with lower fat alternatives (poultry and fish).

Meat is an important source of B-group vitamins, calcium and iron. Because it lacks carbohydrates and vitamin C, meat should be served with starchy, high-fibre foods (pasta, potatoes or vegetables).

STRUCTURE OF MEAT

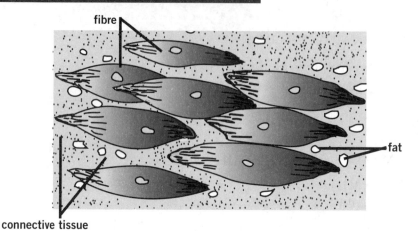

fibre

fat

connective tissue

FACTORS INFLUENCING THE TENDERNESS OF MEAT

- Activity   more active = tougher
                    less active = less tough, more tender

- Age   younger animals tend to be more tender
- Hanging of meat
- Cooking method

TENDERISING MEAT

- Mince or cut into small cubes
- Use a steak hammer or a rolling pin
- Use a chemical tenderiser
- Marinade the pieces of meat
- Use moist, slow-cooking methods (stewing, braising)

GENERAL GUIDELINES FOR CHOOSING AND BUYING MEAT

1 Buy only from a clean, reputable butcher shop or supermarket
2 Meat must be well hung
3 Assistants should not handle meat and money
4 Cooked and raw meats should be displayed, handled and wrapped separately
5 Plastic gloves should be worn by those handling meat; equipment should be kept clean at all times

6   Choose cuts that have a good characteristic colour and smell
7   Meat should be firm and moist
8   Cheaper cuts of meat are just as nutritious as more expensive cuts but need the slower methods of cooking (stewing, etc.)
9   Avoid cuts with too much bone
10 Offal is cheap and nutritious
11 When buying pre-packed meat, check the 'best before' date

RULES FOR STORING MEAT

1   Use fresh meat within two days (check 'best before' date)
2   Unwrap and place on a clean plate, cover and store in the fridge until required
3   Store fresh and cooked meats separately

RULES FOR USING MEAT

1   Remove from fridge as required
2   Do not prepare fresh and cooked meats using the same chopping board or knives
3   Cool cooked meat quickly, cover loosely and put in fridge when cold
4   Cooked meats should be thoroughly reheated if serving them hot
5   Always thaw fully before cooking
6   Do not refreeze thawed meat

EFFECTS OF COOKING ON MEAT

- Micro-organisms are killed
- Colour changes
- Flavour develops
- Collagen changes to gelatine
- Fats melts
- Meat shrinks

Meat can be:

- Boiled
- Roasted
- Stewed
- Braised
- Casseroled
- Stir-fried
- Grilled
- Fried
- Baked
- Steamed

SOME FACTORS AFFECTING CHOICE OF COOKING METHODS

- Equipment
- Time available
- Flavour
- Type of meal
- Cut of meat

MEAT PRODUCTS

Examples of meat products:
Sausages, burgers, meat pies, pâté, samosas, Cornish pasties, white and black puddings, cook–chill products.

POULTRY

TYPES OF POULTRY

Domestic birds: Turkey, chicken, duck, goose
Game birds: Pheasant, duck, grouse, etc.

NUTRITIVE VALUE

Protein:	Good source of HBV protein
Fat:	Low fat content
Carbohydrate:	None present
Vitamins:	Some B-group vitamins, but less than beef, lamb
Minerals:	Calcium and iron
Water:	Amount varies

Poultry is an excellent alternative for people who must reduce the amount of saturated fat in their diet. Most of the fat is located just under the skin. Poultry contains no carbohydrates and is low in minerals and vitamins. It should be served with food combinations rich in carbohydrates, minerals and vitamins. As it is an easily digested food, poultry is suitable for invalids and convalescents.

GENERAL GUIDELINES FOR CHOOSING AND BUYING POULTRY

Fresh:
1 Buy from a clean, reputable shop or supermarket
2 Check the 'use by' label
3 Poultry should be fresh, with white skin and a pleasant smell
4 Avoid poultry that looks discoloured
5 The breast should be plump and the breastbone pliable

Frozen:
1 Poultry must be frozen solid
2 Wrappers must not be damaged
3 Do not buy poultry if it has begun to thaw out

RULES FOR STORING POULTRY

Fresh:
1 Unwrap; remove the giblets
2 Place on a clean plate, loosely cover and put in the fridge
3 Do not store it too close to other foods
4 Cook within two days

Frozen:
1 Put the frozen chicken into the freezer as soon as you return from shopping
2 If the chicken has begun to thaw on the way home, do not refreeze (thaw fully, cook and use)

RULES FOR USING POULTRY

1 Remove fresh poultry from the fridge and wipe dry
2 Remove frozen poultry from the freezer and allow to thaw fully in the fridge before cooking
3 Season with salt, pepper, herbs or garlic
4 Do not stuff the central cavity (cook stuffing separately to avoid problems)

Poultry can be:
- Roasted
- Casseroled
- Steamed
- Boiled
- Grilled
- Stir-fried
- Fried

FISH

Fish can be classified or grouped in three ways:

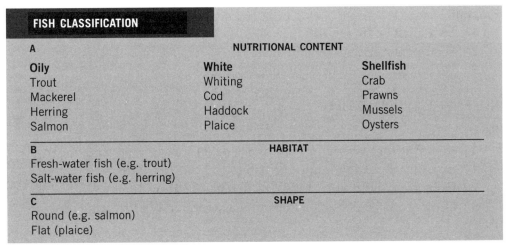

FISH CLASSIFICATION

A — NUTRITIONAL CONTENT		
Oily	**White**	**Shellfish**
Trout	Whiting	Crab
Mackerel	Cod	Prawns
Herring	Haddock	Mussels
Salmon	Plaice	Oysters

B — HABITAT
Fresh-water fish (e.g. trout)
Salt-water fish (e.g. herring)

C — SHAPE
Round (e.g. salmon)
Flat (plaice)

NUTRITIVE VALUE

Protein:	Fish contains almost as much HBV protein as meat
Fat:	Oily fish provides unsaturated fat. Shellfish have a low fat content. In white fish, fat is only found in the liver
Carbohydrate:	None present
Vitamins:	B-group vitamins are in all fish. Oily fish, because of its fat content, also has vitamins A and D
Minerals:	Most fish has iodine, phosphorus and iron. Where bones are eaten (e.g. tinned fish), calcium is present
Water:	Oily fish and shellfish contain less water than white fish

Fish is a good source of HBV protein in an easily digestible form. Fish should be served with carbohydrate-rich food. Oily fish is a good alternative to meat because it provides unsaturated fat. Because of the low fat content of white fish it is suitable for invalids and those on low-fat diets. Oily fish is a good source of fat-soluble vitamins. All fish contain iodine, iron and potassium.

GENERAL GUIDELINES FOR CHOOSING AND BUYING FISH

Fresh:
1 Buy from a clean, reputable shop or supermarket
2 Choose fish that is in season, when it is cheap
3 Fish should be fresh, with eyes bulging, flesh firm, bright red gills and fresh smell
4 Check 'sell by' date (if packed)
5 If wrapped, check that it is not damaged
6 Do not buy fish if it looks discoloured and smells stale

Frozen:
1 Fish must be frozen solid
2 Wrappers must not be damaged
3 Do not buy frozen fish if it looks damaged

RULES FOR STORING FISH

Fresh:
1 Remove from wrapping, put on ice or on a clean plate and cover carefully if putting it into the fridge
2 Do not mix with other foods, as fish has a strong smell
3 Use as soon as possible after purchase (preferably the same day)

Frozen:
1 Put into freezer as soon as possible
2 Never refreeze thawed fish

RULES FOR USING FISH

1 Prepare according to its shape (round, flat)
2 Remove head, bones and fins
3 Rinse and wipe dry

Fish can be:
- Grilled
- Fried
- Baked
- Steamed
- Poached
- Stewed

EFFECTS OF COOKING FISH

- Fish changes colour (from transparent to opaque)
- Protein coagulates and becomes firm
- Cooking dissolves connective tissue
- Vitamins and minerals are dissolved
- Overcooking causes fish to break apart into flakes
- Bacteria are destroyed

PRESERVED FISH

METHOD OF PRESERVING FISH	EXAMPLES
Smoking	Kippers, haddock
Canned	Tuna, salmon
Brine	Prawns, mussels
Frozen	Cod, plaice

EGGS

NUTRITIVE VALUE

Protein:	HBV protein
Fat:	Fat is found in the egg yolks
Carbohydrate:	None present
Minerals:	Iron, calcium, sulphur and phosphorus
Vitamins:	Fat-soluble vitamins A and D, water-soluble vitamin B
Water:	Large amount of water

Eggs provide a useful amount of HBV protein. The fat in the egg yolk is in an easily digested form, but is a saturated fat. It is recommended that we eat no more than seven eggs per week. People with high levels of cholesterol and heart conditions should watch their intake of eggs.

Serve eggs with foods rich in carbohydrates and vitamin C.

STRUCTURE OF EGGS

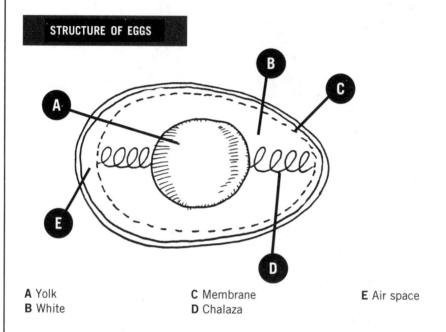

| A Yolk | C Membrane | E Air space |
| B White | D Chalaza | |

USES OF EGGS

USES	EXAMPLES
Binding ingredients	Burgers, rissoles
Coating foods	Fish dipped in egg and breadcrumbs
Eating on their own	Boiled, scrambled, poached, fried, salads
Emulsifying	Mayonnaise
Enriching	Increasing the nutritive value of dishes
Entrapping air	Sponges, meringues
Garnishing	Sieved, sliced on savoury dishes, salads
Glazing	Tarts, scones, pastry flans
Thickening	Quiches, custards

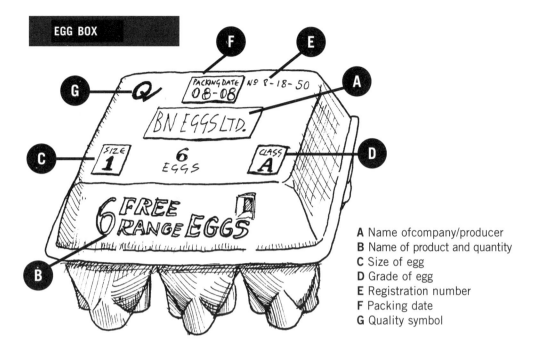

EGG BOX

F PACKING DATE 08-08 E N° 8-18-50 A BN EGGS LTD. C SIZE 1 6 EGGS D CLASS A G Q B 6 FREE RANGE EGGS

A Name ofcompany/producer
B Name of product and quantity
C Size of egg
D Grade of egg
E Registration number
F Packing date
G Quality symbol

GRADING EGGS

SIZE	WEIGHT IN GRAMS
1	70 +
2	65–70
3	60–65
4	55–60
5	50–55
6	45–50
7	< 45

GUIDELINES FOR BUYING EGGS

1 Buy in a busy shop, with a good turnover of customers
2 Check freshness (eggs should be heavy for their size and have a rough shell)
3 Check the label for information about the producer, country of origin, registration number
4 Choose size or class of eggs with dish in mind
5 Number of eggs
6 Check 'best before' date

RULES FOR STORING EGGS AT HOME

1 Store in the fridge with the pointed end down, until required
2 Do not wash the outer shell
3 Avoid storing them near strong-smelling foods
4 Remove from the fridge one hour before using them

RULES FOR USING EGGS

1 Bring to room temperature to get better results when whipping
2 Egg whites should be whisked in bowl free from any trace of fat (including traces of egg yolk)
3 Add hot liquid slowly to eggs to prevent curdling

EFFECTS OF COOKING ON EGGS

- Bacteria are destroyed
- Egg white changes, becomes opaque and hardens
- Protein sets (coagulates)
- Overcooking causes eggs to become indigestible
- If high temperatures are used, eggs will curdle

TESTING FOR FRESHNESS

A Stale   **C** Not so fresh
B Fresh

OMELETTES

Types of omelette:
- Plain
- Soufflé

FILLINGS FOR OMELETTES

SAVOURY	SWEET
Cheese	Jam
Fish	Crushed fruit
Herbs	Cream
Ham	Cream and fruit
Mushroom	
Tomato	

PANCAKES

Types of pancake:
- Sweet
- Savoury

FILLINGS FOR PANCAKES		
SAVOURY		**SWEET**
Chicken	Ham	Crushed fruit
Cheese	Cheese and ham	Stewed fruit
Mushroom	Variety of sauces	Cream

MEAT SUBSTITUTES AND ALTERNATIVES

Examples of meat substitutes and alternatives:
- Nuts
- Pulse vegetables (peas, beans, lentils)
- Quorn (a small plant)
- Soya textured vegetable protein (TVP)

Other alternatives to meat:
- Eggs
- Cheese
- Fish

Uses in the diet:
- Soya products can be used instead of meat or to extend meat dishes (in pies, stews, vegetarian dishes)
- Pulse vegetables are suitable for stews, casseroles, salads, vegetarian dishes
- Nuts added to pies, stuffing and salads will increase the nutritive value without using meat

Advantages of substitutes and alternatives:
- Less expensive than meat
- Intake of saturated animal fat is reduced
- Pulses and soya are rich in protein
- Nutritive value compare well with that of meat
- Soya, pulses, nuts are easy to store
- Saves waste and in some cases saves time
- Some substitutes and alternatives suit vegetarian diets
- New and interesting foods are created
- Interesting dishes can be made from eggs, cheese and fish

Note: When preparing dishes with meat substitutes or alternatives, balance the type of protein (HBV or LBV) by choosing foods that complement each other.

15

STOCKS, SOUPS AND SAUCES

STOCKS

The quality of soups, sauces and gravies is influenced by the quality of the stock used. A stock is the basic liquid used when making soups, sauces and gravies.

Bones, vegetables and/or meat are cooked to extract their flavours during a long, slow cooking time. Stock has a low nutritive value because of the amount of water present.

Stock cubes are a concentrated form of stock and are useful in emergencies. Stock cubes are convenient when time is not available to make stock at home.

SOUPS

As soups have a high water content, their nutritive value is determined by the other ingredients in the soup. Fresh vegetables, meat, poultry, fish, milk and cereals increase the nutritive value of soups. Soups are important in the diet because they stimulate the appetite. They can be served at the start of a meal or used as a snack, for a light lunch or a packed lunch.

CLASSIFICATION OF SOUPS		
CLASS	**TYPE**	**EXAMPLES**
Thick	Purée	Mixed vegetable
	Thickened	Leek and potato
Thin	Clear	Consommé julienne
	Broth	Chicken broth

Others: Chilled soups (e.g. gazpacho), baked soups.

THICKENING SOUPS

Soups can be thickened using:
- Roux: Fat and flour in equal quantities
- Starch: Flour, cornflour, rice, potato
- Egg yolk: Egg yolk and cream (added to rich soups)
- Cereals: Barley, rice

GARNISHES AND ACCOMPANIMENTS FOR SOUP

GARNISH	ACCOMPANIMENT
Croûtons	Melba toast
Cream	Garlic bread
Finely chopped parsley	Brown bread
Chopped chives	Herb bread
Finely grated cheese	Dinner buns, breadsticks

CHARACTERISTICS OF A GOOD SOUP

- Flavoured with the main ingredient
- Fresh ingredients used
- Colour reflects the ingredients used
- Consistency characteristic of the soup
- Piping hot or chilled
- Free from grease
- Well seasoned

COMPARING HOME-MADE SOUP AND CONVENIENCE SOUP

SOUP	ADVANTAGES	DISADVANTAGES
Home-made soup	Fresh ingredients	Takes time to prepare
	Good flavour	Can be more expensive
	Good colour	
	No additives	
Bought soup	Easy to prepare	Flavour can be too strong
	Saves time	Over-seasoned
	Good variety	May contain additives

SAUCES

Sauces may be very simple or elaborate, depending on the dish or type of meal. The ingredients used will determine the nutritive value. Sauces made with water are less nourishing than those containing milk, cream and eggs.

REASONS FOR SERVING SAUCES

Sauces are served with food to:

- Stimulate digestion
- Provide variety of colour, flavour and texture
- Enrich the nutritive value of the food
- Improve the flavour of bland foods
- Counteract the richness of foods

CLASSIFICATION OF SAUCES

CLASSIFICATION	EXAMPLES
Roux	White or Brown
	Béchamel
Cold	Mayonnaise
	Vinaigrette
Egg sauces	Hollandaise
	Custard
Unclassified	Purée (apple, etc.)
	Jam, syrup or fruit sauce

ROUX SAUCES

A roux is equal quantities of fat and flour.
The basic roux sauces are: Pouring, stewing, coating and panard.

ROUX SAUCES

	QUANTITIES			
CONSTITUENT	POURING	STEWING	COATING	PANARD
Fat	25 g	25 g	25 g	25 g
Flour	25 g	25 g	25 g	25 g
Liquid	500 ml	375 ml	250 ml	175 ml

Variation of the basic roux sauce:
- Cheese sauce
- Onion sauce
- Parsley sauce
- Béchamel sauce

CHARACTERISTICS OF A GOOD SAUCE

- Well seasoned
- Correct consistency
- Free from grease
- Flour cooked thoroughly
- Nice flavour

LEFTOVERS

Planning meals carefully will reduce the amount of leftovers. All leftover foods should be used.

Reheated leftovers have a lower nutritive value than food just cooked. Reheated leftovers could cause food poisoning if not reheated correctly or used quickly.

RULES FOR USING LEFTOVERS

1 Reheat food thoroughly to avoid the danger of food poisoning
2 Improve the nutritive value by serving fresh salads and vegetables with leftovers
3 Handle the food as little as possible
4 Use sauces to improve the flavour of leftovers
5 Do not reheat leftovers for a second time
6 Use leftovers within 48 hours – do not store for long. Keep in a cool place, preferably the fridge (never leave in a warm place)

USE OF LEFTOVERS

Leftovers can be used in hot or cold dishes.

EXAMPLES OF USES

FOOD	DISH
Bread	Breadcrumbs, bread sauce, puddings, stuffing, toast
Cakes	Trifle, puddings
Cheese	Grated for toppings, sauces
Egg	Cakes, garnish, glaze, mayonnaise, meringue, salads
Fish	Fish cakes, fish pie, flans, salads, sandwiches
Fruit	Crumble, flans, pies, tarts
Meat	Curry, shepherd's pie, sandwiches, salads

DISHES USING LEFTOVERS

- Meat loaf
- Potato cakes
- Potato croquettes
- Queen of puddings
- Salads
- Shepherd's pie
- Savoury pies
- Trifle
- Vegetable croquettes
- Vol-au-vents (savoury or sweet fillings)

COOKERY TERMS

ACCOMPANIMENT A food or dish which is traditionally served with a particular food or dish (e.g. roast beef and Yorkshire pudding).

AERATING Introducing air into a bread or cake mixture to make it light (e.g. by sieving flour).

À LA CARTE MENU Each dish on the menu is priced separately.

AL DENTE An Italian phrase describing cooked food with a 'bite'.

AU GRATIN Foods cooked in or coated with a sauce sprinkled with breadcrumbs or grated cheese and browned under the grill or in the oven.

AU NATUREL Foods served raw and very simply presented.

BAIN-MARIE A large vessel with about 8 cm of simmering water in which small saucepans or dishes containing food can be kept warm or cooked slowly.

BARBECUE A meal cooked out of doors.

BASTING To pour hot fat or cooking liquid over foods as they are cooking to keep them moist (e.g. hot fat over a roast).

BLANCHING Plunging foods into boiling water to remove skins (from nuts and tomatoes), or to destroy enzymes when preparing vegetables for freezing, or to whiten food.

BOUQUET GARNI A bunch of fresh herbs tied together and used to flavour sauces, soups and stews.

BRINE A mixture of salt and water.

BUFFET A selection of dishes and courses set out on a table with appropriate accompaniments, condiments, plates and cutlery, from which people can help themselves.

CANAPÉS Appetisers of circles or fingers of bread, crackers, pastry, savoury biscuits or toast, with savoury toppings.

CASSEROLE Cooking food slowly in a heat-proof earthenware or Pyrex dish in the oven (e.g. chicken casserole).

CHOWDER	A thick seafood stew.
CONDIMENTS	Salt and pepper.
CONSOMMÉ	A thin clear soup.
CROQUETTE	Potato or minced meat, fish or any savoury mixture, coated with egg and breadcrumbs and deep-fat fried.
CROÛTONS	Diced bread, fried or toasted, served as a garnish or an accompaniment to soup.
CRUDITÉS	Small thin pieces of raw vegetables arranged on a plate and served as hors d'oeuvres.
DICING	Cutting meat or vegetables into small cubes.
DREDGING	Sprinkling flour, caster sugar, spices or herbs over a dish (flour sprinkled over the rolling pin, cinnamon over a rice pudding, castor sugar over apple tart).
FLAN	An open pastry tart or sponge, filled with sweet or savoury ingredients.
GARNISH	A decoration for savoury dishes (sprig of parsley, lemon wedge) to improve the colour and appearance of the dish.
GATEAU	A rich cake decorated and filled (cream and fresh fruit, butter icing and chocolate leaves)
GLAZING	Brushing the tops of pastry and scones with beaten egg, milk, or sugar and water to improve the appearance.
GRATING	Foods thinly cut, using a grater or a food processor (grated cheese, carrot for coleslaw).
HORS D'OEUVRES	Small pieces of savoury foods served before the soup to stimulate the appetite.
INFUSE	Heating herbs, peppercorns, slices of vegetables or strips of lemon or orange rind in a liquid to flavour it.
LIAISON	A thickening or binding substance used when making sauces, soups and stews.
MARINADE	Oil, seasonings, wine and vinegar mixed together. It is used to flavour and tenderise meat by steeping the meat in the liquid, before cooking.

PANARD	A very thick sauce made from fat, flour and liquid. It is used to bind ingredients.
PARBOIL	Half cooking food by boiling and then finishing cooking using another method.
PETIT FOURS	Small fancy cakes.
PULSES	Pulse vegetables (peas, beans, lentils).
PURÉE	A smooth mixture of fish, fruit, meat or vegetables which has been sieved.
ROUX	A mixture of equal quantities of fat and flour cooked together, used as a basis for sauces (pouring, stewing, coating, panard).
SAUTÉING	Frying food quickly in a small amount of hot fat or oil (sautéed potatoes).
SEASONING	Adding salt, pepper, herbs or spices to improve the flavour of a dish.
SHORTENING	Fats used when making breads and cakes.
SWEAT	To cook vegetables in a small amount of melted fat.
SYRUP	Sugar added to water to make a concentrated solution.
ZEST	The outer skin of oranges and lemons containing the essential oils which produce the flavour.

18

CONSUMER EDUCATION

WHAT IS CONSUMER EDUCATION?

Consumer education provides consumers with the opportunity to develop their decision-making skills in order to prioritise when choosing goods and services. Consumers gain valuable information and skills which can then be used in everyday situations.

WHO ARE CONSUMERS?

People who buy or use services and goods are called consumers.

WHAT IS AN INFORMED CONSUMER?

A person who knows their responsibilities and rights when they buy services and goods is an informed consumer. An informed consumer should know about consumer responsibilities, laws, product labelling, quality, etc.

SERVICES

Services are used; goods (food, clothing, etc.) are consumed or worn.
All consumers use services.

SERVICES USED BY CONSUMERS		
LOCAL	**STATE**	**VOLUNTARY**
Schools	Education	Vincent de Paul
Hospitals	Health	ISPCC
Post	Communications	Red Cross
Gardaí	Justice	Youth clubs
Residence associations		

Other services: Gas, electricity, water, telephones, public library, public transport, roads, public lighting.

GOODS USED BY CONSUMERS

Houses, food, furniture, books, stereos, petrol, central heating oil, water for washing clothes.

DIRECT AND INDIRECT SERVICES

DIRECT SERVICES	INDIRECT SERVICES
Dry cleaning	Roads
Hairdressers	Public lighting
Supermarkets	An Post
Cinemas	Libraries
Laundries	Parks

CHARACTERISTICS OF GOOD SERVICE

- Clean, well-organised and efficient premises
- A friendly atmosphere
- Helpful, friendly and efficient staff
- Short queues
- Good facilities for people with disabilities
- Immediate attention

NEEDS, WANTS AND LUXURIES

WHAT IS A NEED?

A need is something we must have to survive and live.
Examples: Food, housing, warmth, clothing, water.

WHAT IS A WANT?

A want is something we desire but do not need to survive. Some wants might be considered as needs by individuals, depending on their priorities (e.g. a car to get to work).
Examples: Car, holiday, designer clothes, walkman, stereo.

WHAT IS A LUXURY?

A luxury is not essential for survival. Luxuries are the extras in life which money can buy. Depending on money available, chocolate could be considered a luxury in some situations.
Examples: Extra clothes, fillet steak, gold, expensive furniture and furnishings, two cars, new shrubs for the garden, books.

Note: Needs, wants and luxuries vary from family to family, due to different circumstances, priorities and values.

DECISION-MAKING (SELECTING GOODS AND SERVICES)

Many factors affect the way goods and services are chosen by consumers. We use our decision-making skills to make the best choice.

Decision-making is influenced by:
- Priorities and values
- Needs and wants
- Age
- Peer influence in relation to trends
- Gender
- Resources available
- Where we live (location)
- Advertising
- Social implications of the choice
- Time available to make the choice

CONSUMER RESPONSIBILITIES

Consumers are entitled to certain rights under law but they also have responsibilities as consumers. Consumers must:
- Be informed
- Become familiar with consumer laws
- Read labels about services and on goods before using them
- Examine a product before buying it
- Understand symbols and warnings on the labels
- Use the product according to the manufacturer's instructions
- Use the product for the task intended

CONSUMER RIGHTS AND PROTECTION

CONSUMER RIGHTS

Informed consumers are aware of their rights to:
- Accurate information
- Choose
- High-quality services and goods
- Value for money
- High standards of safety
- Redress

CONSUMER INFORMATION

Information provided must be accurate and clear. It must not be misleading or false.

Sources of consumer information:
- The Consumer Association of Ireland
- The Office of Consumer Affairs and Fair Trade
- The Ombudsman
- The Irish Goods Council
- Consumer education in schools
- Labelling, date stamping, unit pricing, instructions
- Symbols on products
- Advertising
- Newspapers, magazines, leaflets
- Shops and showrooms
- Consumer programmes on television and radio
- Friends (word-of-mouth)

CONSUMER CHOICE

Consumers can choose from a variety of products and services provided by different manufacturers and providers who are in competition with each other. If a company has a monopoly they may not feel obliged to offer competitive prices. Consumers can make demands which raise the quality and increase the range of goods and services available.

QUALITY

Quality guarantees that services and goods are of a high standard.

QUALITY CONTROL

Quality control or testing is carried out by the manufacturers of goods and providers of services to assure the consumer of the quality.

QUALITY MANAGEMENT

Quality management encourages manufacturers and providers of services to continually improve their products and services to meet consumer demands.

STANDARDS OF SAFETY

Consumers are entitled to safe goods and services.

SYMBOLS AND MARKS

Symbols on toys, furniture, food, clothing and electrical goods indicate that they have been tested. Hazardous chemicals, materials and goods carry symbols, information and instructions on how they should be used.

QUALITY SYMBOLS

 (a) Approved Quality System/Quality Irish

 (g) Flame resistant

 (b) Guaranteed Irish

 (h) Doubly insulated

 (c) Communauté Européenne

 (i) BSI safety mark

 (d) Design Centre

 **(j)** Irish mark of electrical conformity

 (e) Caighdean Éireannach/ Irish Standards Mark

 (k) Recyclable

 (f) BSI kitemark

 (l) Office of Consumer Affairs

HAZARDOUS SUBSTANCES OR MATERIALS

 (a) Harmful and irritant

 (c) Flammable

 (b) Toxic

 (d) Corrosive

VALUE FOR MONEY

Value for money means that the consumer pays the appropriate price for services and goods, based on their true quality. Sale items are only bargains when first-quality items are reduced in price and the consumer needs them.

RIGHT OF REDRESS

It is the consumers' responsibility to know:
- Their rights and laws covering such rights
- How to make a complaint
- Where to go to make the complaint

CONSUMER PROTECTION – THE CONSUMER LAWS

CONSUMER INFORMATION ACT 1978

This Act states that it is an offence for providers of services or manufacturers of goods to:
- Advertise misleading or false claims about the price
- Make misleading claims about price reductions
- Create false claims about services or goods
- Display an advert that might mislead consumers

The Consumer Information Act 1978 also demands that prices should be clearly visible in the shop.

THE SALE OF GOODS AND SUPPLY OF SERVICES ACT 1980

This Act states that goods should be:

- Of merchantable quality (in perfect condition)
- Fit or suitable for the task or purpose (can do the job)
- As described in the advert, on the label, etc.
- The same as samples displayed in the store

The Sale of Goods and Supply of Services Act 1980 also indicates that shops may not put up notices which attempt to interfere with consumer rights.

Examples:

ONLY CREDIT NOTES GIVEN

NO REFUNDS GIVEN

GOODS WILL NOT BE EXCHANGED

NO LIABILITY FOR FAULTY GOODS

SALE GOODS CANNOT BE EXCHANGED

The Sale of Goods and Services Act 1980 covers the provision of services. Consumers are entitled to have the service provided by suppliers, using skilled or qualified staff, quality materials and paying attention to care, diligence and safety.

CONSUMER PROTECTION — GUARANTEES

Under a guarantee, manufacturers or retailers declare that all faults that develop during the period of the guarantee will be fixed and faulty goods will be replaced. A guarantee is a contract between the seller and the buyer, but it can be extended to include a person who receives an item as a gift.

WHAT IS A QUOTATION?

A quotation is a written, itemised, fixed price for a job.

WHAT IS AN ESTIMATE?

An estimate is a general rough price for a job. Usually it is not written down.

CONSUMER ACTION

If a consumer has a valid complaint about a product, there are certain guidelines which should be followed. A contract exists between the consumer and the retailer. The retailer must deal with the complaint.

LIMITING CONSUMER RIGHTS

Consumers can limit their own rights by not following the manufacturer's instructions or deciding that they do not like the colour, etc., when they get home.

GUIDELINES WHEN MAKING COMPLAINTS

1   Do not use the product if you notice a fault.
2   Stop using the product if it develops a fault when in use.
3   Return the product and the receipt to the shop immediately.
4   Explain the nature of the problem. Produce the receipt and the product.
5   If the assistant cannot help, ask to speak to the manager or supervisor.
6   Keep to the facts and calmly ask what the retailer will do to solve the problem.

Solutions might involve replacement, refund or repair. If the complaint is valid and is in breach of the consumer laws, a consumer is not obliged to accept a credit note.

GENERAL GUIDELINES FOR COMPLAINING IN WRITING

If the problem is not solved, put the complaint in writing to the manager or director, outlining clearly:
- The item purchased (manufacturer's name, make and model)
- The date of purchase
- A copy of the receipt of purchase (keep the original receipt)
- The nature of the problem
- The return visit to the shop and the name of the person spoken to
- The action you expect the company to take

Be polite at all times, whether complaining in person, by phone or in writing. Keep a copy of letters written.

TAKING FURTHER ACTION

If the visit to the shop and the letter do not produce a satisfactory solution, the consumer may have to consider contacting relevant consumer organisations and taking legal action.

ORGANISATIONS AND AGENCIES

CONSUMER ASSOCIATION OF IRELAND

The Consumer Association of Ireland provides:
- Information on consumer affairs
- A Consumer Personal Service which advises consumers
- A consumer magazine, *Consumer Choice*

THE OMBUDSMAN

The Ombudsman provides help for consumers who wish to make complaints against a government agency (e.g. An Post).

DIRECTOR OF CONSUMER AFFAIRS

The Director of Consumer Affairs:
- Enforces laws relating to the sale of goods and services
- Controls standards of advertising
- Encourages higher standards relating to goods and services

SMALL CLAIMS COURT

The Small Claims Court hears consumer complaints in relation to claims of up to £500 (e.g. poor service, inadequate workmanship, faulty goods).

TRADE ASSOCIATIONS

Trade Associations encourage the development of higher standards among their members.

Examples of Trade Associations:
- Licensed Vintners' Association
- RGDATA (grocers/shopkeepers)

CONSUMERS AND ADVERTISING

Advertising is used to sell goods and services. It carries a message for the consumer.

FUNCTIONS OF ADVERTISING

- To sell products or services
- To promote new products and make them popular

- To create a healthy, environmentally friendly image
- To promote the company
- To increase sales

ADVANTAGES OF ADVERTISING

- Provides information
- Creates interest in goods and services
- Sells goods and services
- Encourages competition and may reduce prices of certain items
- Provides employment

DISADVANTAGES OF ADVERTISING

- Cost of advertising is included in the cost of the product
- Intrudes into people's lives
- Can reinforce stereotyping
- Creates a desire in people to buy products they cannot afford
- Encourages consumerism

CONTROLLING ADVERTISING STANDARDS

Control is exercised by a voluntary organisation, the Advertising Standards Authority for Ireland. This body encourages all advertisers to create 'legal, decent, honest and truthful' advertisements.

Legal control is exercised by:
- Employment Equality Act 1977
- The Consumer Information Act 1978
- The EC Misleading Advertising Directive

POPULAR ADVERTISING MEDIA

- Television, radio
- Cinema
- Magazines, newspapers
- Directories, direct mail
- Billboards
- Clothing (tee-shirts, jeans, runners, etc.)
- Sponsorship of public events
- Bus shelters
- Window displays and shop displays
- Products (labels, posters, pens, key-ring holders, etc.)

IMAGES USED IN ADVERTISING

To persuade consumers to buy, specific images are used to promote goods and services. These could be any of the following:

- Humour, comedy
- Environmental considerations
- The perfect family
- Healthy outdoor people
- Romance
- Luxurious lifestyle
- Glamorous people
- Experts providing advice

Techniques also used include the use of music, bright colours, idyllic locations and catchy phrases.

MARKETING

WHAT IS MARKETING?

Marketing uses the information gathered from market research to design advertisements to target the right group of consumers.

WHAT IS MARKET RESEARCH?

To find out what people like, market research companies carry out surveys for advertisers. Sometimes questionnaires are used as part of a survey to gather information.

MARKET RESEARCH TECHNIQUES

Selected samples of consumers are:

- Surveyed personally (on the street, by phone)
- Interviewed on the street
- Surveyed individually by post

19

BUDGETING

DEFINITIONS

A BUDGET is a personal plan for saving and spending money. It balances income and expenditure.

INCOME is the money earned from work done and from investments.

EXPENDITURE is money spent out of income. Examples of expenditure are rent, mortgage, food, clothing, energy, entertainment, savings, toiletries, gifts, travel.

GROSS INCOME is income earned before tax and other items are deducted.

DEDUCTIONS are taxes, PRSI and voluntary deductions (pension, health or saving schemes, etc.)

NET INCOME is the money left after deductions.

MONEY MANAGEMENT SYSTEM

A good money manager will:
- Look at the resources available
- Decide on the goal
- Make out a budget
- Put the budget into action
- Evaluate the budget
- Make adjustments

PLANNING A PERSONAL BUDGET

WRITE IT DOWN

- Identify personal needs and priorities
- List income and all sources of income
- List expenditure, expenses and savings
- Examine income and expenditure
- Make out the budget
- Put the budget into action
- Evaluate the results
- Revise the budget when necessary

EXAMINING A BUDGET

QUESTIONS TO ASK

- Do income and expenditure balance?
- Have you overspent?
- Did you borrow money or use an overdraft facility?
- Did you save money?
- Do you need to reorganise spending?

PLANNING A HOUSEHOLD BUDGET

WRITE IT DOWN

- List all family needs
- List all family income and sources of income
- List all expenditure (fixed, irregular, variable)
- Examine income and expenditure
- Make out the budget
- Put the budget into action
- Evaluate what has happened
- Revise budget when necessary

EXAMPLES OF EXPENDITURE

FIXED	IRREGULAR	VARIABLE
Rent	Food	Savings
Mortgage	Energy	Gifts
Repayments	Electricity	Pastimes and hobbies
Insurances	Clothing	Entertainment
	Transport	Household
	Telephone	Holidays
	TV licence	Pocket money

ADVANTAGES OF BUDGETING

- Reduces financial worries
- Income and expenditure can be balanced
- Prevents overspending on wants and luxuries

- Arrangement for larger bills can be made (electricity, telephone, etc.)
- Encourages saving for seasonal spending (Christmas)
- Encourages saving for holidays, the 'rainy day', education
- Budgeting is a good discipline for all the family
- Budgeting controls use of ATM cards

Family budgets must be revised regularly and be flexible, to cope with bills and changing family needs.

20

SHOPPING

Each local area provides consumers with a variety of shops. Some areas have more variety than others.

TYPES OF SHOPS OR OUTLETS

Some large shops are found only in cities or large towns. Smaller shops may be located in suburban or rural areas. Chain shops may be found in larger towns and cities.

SUPERMARKETS

These are self-service outlets stocking food and small household items. Own- brand products are available in some supermarkets. **Examples:** Superquinn, Quinnsworth.

DEPARTMENT STORES

These are large shopping areas divided into a number of smaller areas or units, each selling particular products or brands of similar products. Examples of products include clothing, footwear, cosmetics, electrical equipment, furniture and fabrics. Many department stores provide toilet and restaurant facilities for customers. **Examples:** Arnotts, Clerys.

MULTI CHAIN STORES

Several shops of retail chains are located around the country, each providing the same range of goods arranged in the same way. Shops are almost exactly the same. **Examples:** Dunnes Stores, Penneys.

INDEPENDENT CHAIN SHOPS

Shops belonging to this group are independently or individually owned. They are small supermarkets and grocery shops. **Examples:** Mace, Spar, Centra, Super Valu.

HYPERMARKETS

These are large warehouse buildings selling a vast range of goods. They are generally situated in the suburbs.

SPECIALIST SHOPS

These shops sell a specific category of goods, such as bread and cakes, foods, clothes, jewellery, electrical goods, books, shoes.

DISCOUNT SHOPS

Discount shops provide consumers with a small range of goods which are reduced in price (electrical, gifts, etc.)

OTHER SHOPPING OUTLETS

- Markets
- Auction rooms
- Door-to-door selling
- Parties
- Vending machines
- Mail order

MODERN SELF-SERVICE SHOPS

Advantages:
- Convenient and fast for those with little time
- Fast turnover of foods ensures freshness
- Goods on display can be easily seen
- Large range of goods available
- Extensive variety of brand names
- Own brands available in some stores
- Lower prices than in very small shops

Disadvantages:
- Impersonal compared to smaller shops
- Generally not open on Sundays
- Queues frequently occur
- No credit facilities
- Danger of impulse buying

COUNTER SERVICE SHOPS

Advantages:
- Personal, friendly service by people known to consumer
- Credit facilities on offer in some small shops
- Advice is freely given
- Open late and on Sundays

Disadvantages:
- Smaller variety of goods
- Displays of goods limited
- Higher overheads result in higher prices
- Can be time-consuming to shop

TECHNIQUES TO ENCOURAGE CONSUMER SPENDING

- Attractive background music
- Interesting colours
- Aroma of freshly cooked foods (breads, meats, etc.)
- Wide aisles for ease of movement around the shop
- Essentials at the back of the shop or on lower shelves
- You pass luxury items (sweets, etc.) to get to essentials
- Luxury goods positioned on shelves at eye level or just above
- Sweets, magazines and special offers at the checkouts
- Food sampling on late-night opening

METHODS OF PAYING BILLS

- Cash
- Credit card (Visa, Access, American Express)
- Cheque and cheque card
- ATM card (Cashcard, Pass, Banklink)

GENERAL GUIDELINES FOR SHOPPING

- Never shop for food when hungry
- Make a shopping list for the week and stick to the list

- Choose shops that are hygienic and well organised, where food is stored correctly
- Shop where staff follow the rules for personal hygiene and food hygiene
- Demand quality and a good aftersales service
- Shop around and be familiar with the goods on the market
- Compare prices and quantities for different brands
- Do not buy damaged foods or goods
- Check 'best before' date
- Keep all receipts

SHOPPING TERMS

Own brands   Some outlets sell products with their own name on them in simple packaging. They are generally cheaper than branded products.

Unit pricing   Fruits, vegetables, cheese and some other foods are sold according to cost per unit weight.

Loss leaders   To encourage people to come into a particular shop, goods are sold at a loss in the hope that they will complete their shopping there.

Bulk buying   Consumers buy goods in large amounts because they are cheaper. They are not good value for money if you do not need them.

PACKAGING

EXAMPLES OF PACKAGING

TYPES	ADVANTAGES	DISADVANTAGES
Plastic	Variety available Can be recycled Easy to clean Strong	Can taint food Non-biodegradable
Paper	A variety of uses Can be recycled Biodegradable Clean	Not strong Reduces the forests
Glass	Strong Hygienic Easy to clean Can be recycled	Can break easily Dangerous if it splinters
Cans	Can be recycled Hygienic	Can rust Food can be contaminated

Examples of uses

Foods	Packaging
Eggs	Paper or plastic cartons
Juices	Lined wax paper cartons, glass, cans
Jams	Glass jars
Milk	Lined wax cartons, glass
Cream	Plastic tubs
Cereals	Waxed paper
Bread	Unwrapped, in plastic covers or wax paper
Meat	Plastic bags
Sauces	Waxed sachets, glass jars, cans

21

MANAGEMENT

WHAT IS MANAGEMENT?

Management involves setting goals, examining resources, making decisions, taking action and evaluating the results.

WHAT IS RESOURCE MANAGEMENT?

Resource management is controlling and using all the resources available to gain the most from them.

WHAT IS HOME MANAGEMENT?

Home management applies the same principles of management. It involves the use of the resources available to implement the goals (keeping the home running effectively and efficiently).

WHAT IS TIME MANAGEMENT?

Time management is concerned with organising the time available to implement and complete goals in an efficient way so that there is free time left to do other things (leisure pursuits). Time is not wasted.

MANAGERS

Examples of managers
- Principal of a school
- Bank manager
- Managing director of a company
- Factory manager
- Farm manager
- Home manager

GOALS

WHAT ARE GOALS?

Goals can be defined as the tasks or aims we set for ourselves. Goals will be different, depending on the resources available to the person.

TYPES OF GOALS

GOAL	EXAMPLE
Short term	Washing and ironing
Medium term	Saving for a new CD player
Long term	Buying a house

RESOURCES

RESOURCES AVAILABLE

These include:
- Human resources
- Knowledge and skills
- Time
- Energy
- Money

COMMUNITY RESOURCES

- Agencies and organisations
- Schools
- Libraries
- State services (postal service, etc.)

WHAT ARE COMMODITIES?

Examples of commodities include:
- Labour-saving equipment
- Food
- Electricity and gas

EXAMPLES OF PERSONAL RESOURCES

- Skills
- Time
- Money available
- Knowledge
- Energy
- Equipment in the home

Resources which could be limited in the home are money, time, energy, equipment, skills or knowledge.

Resources that money can buy include equipment, people's skills and knowledge, time, information.

MANAGEMENT SYSTEMS

A good management system involves the following steps:
1 Identify and set the goal or aim
2 Identify the resources available and other resources that might be needed
3 Make a plan and include the time plan
4 Implement the plan (take action)
5 Evaluate the plan
6 Modify the plan

EFFECTS OF GOOD MANAGEMENT SYSTEMS ON THE FAMILY

A good management system affects the family by ensuring that:
- Resources are allocated effectively
- Household tasks get done efficiently
- Money is not wasted
- Time is available for leisure pursuits, etc.
- Resources can be reallocated after evaluating the plan
- Everyone in the family can be involved

WORK PLANS

Involve the whole family when organising work plans. Divide the tasks to be done into daily, weekly and seasonal categories. Organise tasks to suit individual skills and time at work or school.

Tasks such as washing dishes, washing and ironing clothes and vacuuming can be done using a rota system. Try to get one or two of the weekly jobs done each day.

HOME MANAGEMENT TASKS CHART

DAILY	WEEKLY	OCCASIONALLY
Washing up	Ironing	Painting
Dusting	Vacuuming	Christmas cakes
Tidying rooms	Gardening	Washing windows

WHAT IS TIME AND MOTION STUDY?

Time and motion study involves evaluating how much time and energy is required to achieve goals and complete tasks. Records are kept of everything that needs to be done to complete a task.

WORK ROUTINES FOR HOUSEHOLD CLEANING

CASE STUDY A

Design a general work routine for cleaning a room.

General plan of action (adapt to any room):
1 Collect all the equipment needed to put the plan into action (cloths, cleaning agents, brush, duster, vacuum cleaner, etc.)
2 Open windows to let fresh air into the room
3 Tidy (collect newspapers, empty bin, hang up clothes, make beds, tidy cushions, books, etc.)
4 Clean out fireplace if there is one in the room
5 Sweep the room at this stage, if it has smooth flooring
6 Dust all surfaces using a damp cloth
7 Vacuum, if the room has not been swept
8 Wash windows, doors, skirtings and windowsills
9 Polish furniture and other surfaces

CASE STUDY B

Devise a list of guidelines for general cleaning. Make a list of the cleaning agents used in the home.

General guidelines:
1 Be organised
2 Collect all the resources needed (equipment, cleaning agents, cloths, etc.)
3 In any room, clean from the higher surfaces to the lower surfaces
4 Do not use harsh cleaning agents
5 Follow the 'general plan of action', as above

HOME HYGIENE

BASIC RULES FOR HOME HYGIENE

1 Ventilate the house every morning (open all the windows)
2 Maintain even temperatures throughout the house to prevent damp
3 Clean the kitchen and bathroom daily
4 Keep all surfaces washed
5 Wash kitchen cloths, tea towels and bathroom towels daily
6 Make beds and tidy the bedroom
7 Clean out fireplaces, tidy and dust the living-room
8 Vacuum the whole house once or twice a week
9 Keep drains clean and disinfect regularly
10 Wash and dry the kitchen bin every day
11 Each week wash, disinfect and dry the outdoor bin

CLEANING AGENTS

Natural cleaning agents: Vinegar, lemon juice.

Keep the cleaning agents in one press away from children, food, equipment, dishes and saucepans. Mark all cleaning agents clearly. Do not remove from the original container.

CLEANING AGENTS CHART

CLEANING AGENT	EXAMPLE	USES
Bleach	Parazone	Stains on surfaces
Detergent	Bold	Washing clothes
Disinfectant	Dettol	Work surfaces
Non-abrasive cleaner	Jif	Sinks, work surfaces
Polish	Pledge	Furniture
	Silvo	Silver
	Klear	Floors
Wash-up liquid	Morning Fresh	Dishes, glasses
Liquid cleaner	Windolene	Windows, mirrors

Choosing cleaning agents:
1 Read the label
2 Is it for one cleaning task or is it a multipurpose cleaning agent?
3 Is it an environmentally friendly product?
4 What ingredients are in it?

5 Will it damage the surface?
6 What are its advantages and disadvantages?
7 Are there any warning symbols or information on the product?
8 Are instructions for its use clear?
9 Is it value for money?
10 How is it packaged (aerosol, cardboard box, plastic)?

22

HOME STUDIES

WHAT IS SHELTER?

Shelter is a home which protects us from the elements (wind, rain, etc.) and provides us with a safe, secure and private environment in which to live. In early times, human beings also needed protection from wild animals.

WHAT IS A HOME?

A home is the friendly, familiar, warm, comfortable and safe place where we live.

Traditional homes of the world:
- Cottage
- Bamboo hut
- Tent
- Houseboat
- Igloo
- Caravan

Modern types of home:
- Detached house
- Semi-detached house
- Apartment or flat
- Maisonette
- Sheltered complex
- Bungalow
- Terraced house

Homes can be:
- Temporary or permanent
- Rented or owned
- Privately owned or local authority owned

MEETING HUMAN NEEDS

The home meets basic human needs. These are:
- Physical (protection from the elements)
- Social (a place for family, friends and people with special needs in society, such as the elderly, etc.)
- Emotional (a place where we feel comfortable and safe; a private place in which to relax)

GENERAL GUIDELINES FOR CHOOSING A HOME

Some of the factors which influence people when choosing a home are:
- Money
- Location
- Type and size of home
- Transport
- Distance from facilities (schools, shops, hospital, library)
- Town or country
- Safety

Some people choose to buy rather than rent, because they consider the house as a long-term investment which will increase in value over time.

23

DESIGN PRINCIPLES IN THE HOME

WHAT IS DESIGN?

A design is a plan featuring a structure, with all the lines and shapes which make up the structure.

WHAT IS A DESIGNER?

A designer is the person who creates the design and provides the plan to implement the design.

WHAT IS THE DESIGN PROCESS?

The design process is the plan of action followed to create the design.

DESIGN IN HOME ECONOMICS

Design is a part of many aspects of home economics and influences our lives in many ways.

DESIGN IN THE HOME		
AREA	**EXAMPLE**	**END PRODUCT**
Interior design	Room planning	Kitchen layout
Textiles	Soft furnishings	Curtains
Equipment	Labour saving	Food processor
Services	Electricity	Plugs
Food	Meal planning	Garnishes

FACTORS INVOLVED IN GOOD DESIGN

The basic factors of good design are function, appearance, quality and durability.

DESIGN PRINCIPLES

Good design follows certain basic rules. Designers make use of three design principles to achieve satisfactory results.

PROPORTION

Designs should be in proportion (small items of furniture in small rooms, mirrors in proportion to the fireplace, fireplace in proportion to the size of the room).

EMPHASIS

If a room or an object has a special feature that provides a focus in the design (fireplace, mirror, painting, small table), it is called emphasis of design.

BALANCE

This is achieved by arranging colours, patterns, textures, lines, shapes, proportion and emphasis in a way that is pleasing to the eye. A harmony is achieved in the design.

BASIC ELEMENTS OF DESIGN

The design of anything is determined by the basic elements of design. By balancing each with the other, a pleasing design may be created. The basic elements are:

- Colour
- Pattern
- Line
- Shape
- Texture

COLOUR

Colour is an important aspect of our environment. It is all around us, we also wear colour and we are affected psychologically by the colours we see.

Colours can appear warm or cold. Pale colours make rooms appear bigger. Darker colours make rooms appear smaller.

COLOUR CHART A

Primary	Mixing primary		Secondary colours
Red	Red + Yellow	→	Orange
Yellow	Red + Blue	→	Purple
Blue	Yellow + Blue	→	Green

COLOUR CHART B

Warm colours	Cool colours
Red	Blue
Yellow	Green
Orange	

Choose warm colours for north facing rooms and cooler colours for south facing rooms.

Neutral colours: White, grey.

Shades: When black is added to any colour, a shade is created.
Tints: When white is added to any colour, a tint results.

PATTERN

Pattern is used by designers to break up the plain surfaces on which they work their design. Pattern introduces interest. It contrasts strongly with the plain surfaces around it. Pattern can be used as a design feature by the designer.

Types of pattern:

- Geometric
- Floral
- Motifs
- Trellis
- Self-patterned
- Period style

General guidelines for using pattern:
- In small rooms use small patterns and choose large patterns for larger rooms.
- The same pattern can sometimes be used on different surfaces (wall covering and curtains).
- Where two patterns are used, one should be larger than the other.
- Avoid patterns that create visual clutter.

TEXTURE

A room with only one texture is boring. 'Texture' describes the smoothness or the roughness of any surface. A variety of textures is more pleasing to the eye. Some textures are suited to particular surfaces because of their characteristics (easy to clean, etc.)

Examples of texture

Soft	Hard	Rough	Smooth
Carpet	Brick	Brick	Marble
Towels	Marble	Carpet	Glass
Curtains	Wood	Towels	Stainless steel

General guidelines for using texture:
- Choose smooth textures for kitchens and bathrooms, as they are easy to clean and do not encourage bacteria.
- Avoid having too many smooth textures in the living-room, as they can look too clinical.
- Choose a mixture of rough, smooth and soft textures for balance.
- Rough textures look more comfortable than soft textures.

SHAPE

The basic shapes used in design are square, rectangular, triangular and circular. All items have a shape. Some combine shapes.

LINE

Four types of line are used in design. Line influences the design.

Vertical: These lines draw the eye up and down walls, rooms and objects. Rooms appear visually higher, objects appear taller.

Horizontal: These lines draw the eye across the room. Horizontal lines make rooms look wider. There is less emphasis on height.

Curved lines: Rooms or objects with curved lines look softer. They are easier on the eye.

Diagonal: Lines crossing at the diagonal are used less frequently. They create a visual impact whether on a wall, fabric or in furniture design. Diagonal lines must be used with care.

DESIGN AND ROOM PLANNING

Design in the home aims to create a comfortable environment where people can relax and enjoy being at home. The functional aspects of a home are looked after in a well-designed home (room planning, furniture, lighting, heating, electricity).

GENERAL GUIDELINES FOR ROOM PLANNING

Consider each of the following:
- Function of the room (kitchen, living-room, etc.)
- Space available (space for furniture and storage)
- Aspect of the room (this influences colour schemes)
- Storage space (for now and the future)
- Services (heating, lighting, electricity, ventilation)
- Type and size of furniture for the room
- Space between furniture
- Position of doors and traffic flow
- Safety
- Hygiene

WHAT IS TRAFFIC FLOW?

Traffic flow is the movement of people within the room, between furniture and the door and around pieces of furniture.

PRIORITIES

The type of room will determine the priorities when planning rooms. Priorities could be some or all of the following:

Safety • Appearance • Comfort • Services • Colour scheme

Efficiency • Storage • Hygiene • Function • Texture

THE DESIGN PROCESS

The design process can be applied to room planning, as well as many other areas.

OUTLINE OF DESIGN PROCESS

1 Design brief (e.g. plan a new kitchen)
2 Analyse the task
3 Research possible solutions and the resources needed
4 Limit the ideas to a few and consider these carefully
5 Choose one idea as the solution to the problem
6 Draw a plan of action
7 Implement the plan
8 Evaluate the results

KITCHEN PLANNING

The modern kitchen is planned so that all activities are carried out efficiently. The study of people and their surroundings is called 'ergonomics'. Kitchens can be U-shaped, L-shaped or galley in design.

SEQUENCE OF ACTIVITIES

A natural sequence of activities takes place in the kitchen which determines the layout of the work units and the position of large appliances (storage, food preparation, cooking, serving and washing up).

ARRANGEMENT OF KITCHEN UNITS AND EQUIPMENT

FUNCTION	WHERE
Food storage area	Cupboards, work surface, fridge
Food preparation area	Work surface, cupboards, sink, dishwasher
Cooking area	Work surfaces on both sides of the cooker
Serving area	Work surface.

WHAT IS THE WORK TRIANGLE?

The three large pieces of equipment (fridge, cooker and sink) are arranged in an imaginary triangle. It is called the 'work triangle'. The triangle should not measure more than seven metres. If the three pieces of equipment are too close to each other, the kitchen will be cramped. If the triangle is very large, it leads to extra walking to perform tasks.

GOOD KITCHEN DESIGN

A well-designed kitchen is safe, well lit, well ventilated, comfortable, with easy-to-clean surfaces and equipment.

Kitchens sometimes need to be designed for people with special needs (e.g. someone in a wheelchair, a blind person). Their needs will be different. They need to be able to move around and work safely and comfortably in the kitchen (unit heights may need to be altered to cater for someone in a wheelchair).

SUITABLE SURFACES FOR KITCHENS

Work units: Modern, easy-to-clean melamine work surfaces with wood and man-made surfaces on doors. Hygienic surfaces are important in kitchens.

Flooring: Vinyl is easy to clean, comfortable and reasonably hard-wearing. Tiles are also easy to clean and hard-wearing, but they are not comfortable for standing on for a long time.

Wall covering: Washable paint, spongeable or vinyl wall coverings and tiles are suitable for the kitchen.

24

SAFETY IN THE HOME

Some accidents which occur in the home can be prevented, and the risk of others can be reduced.

SOME CAUSES OF ACCIDENTS IN THE HOME

- Badly designed homes, equipment and rooms
- Incorrectly installed equipment
- Faulty equipment
- A child's curiosity
- An elderly person's slow reactions
- Mixing water and electricity
- Falls
- Fires (e.g. deep-fat fryers)

PREVENTION OF ACCIDENTS

STAIRS AND STEPS

- Ensure that stairs and steps have adequate lighting

- Safety gates should be used on stairs, where there are toddlers
- Keep stairs and steps free of toys

FIRE

- Use a firescreen in front of fires
- Empty ashtrays
- Never leave deep-fat fryers unattended
- Install smoke alarms
- Install a fire extinguisher and fire blanket
- Close all internal doors at night

ELECTRICITY

- Never use faulty equipment
- Never handle electrical switches or appliances with wet hands
- Never take an electrical appliance into the bathroom
- Install pull cords in bathrooms (place light switches outside the bathroom door)
- Avoid trailing flexes in rooms
- Unplug the television and other appliances at night

GENERAL SAFETY MEASURES

- Use non-slip mats in baths and showers
- Avoid putting rugs on highly polished floors
- Replace worn floor coverings
- Install adequate lighting throughout the house
- Do not overload sockets
- Store all chemicals in a cupboard out of the reach of children
- Keep all knives in a safe drawer out of the reach of children
- Use child-proof locks on kitchen units

ORGANISATIONS RESPONSIBLE FOR COMMUNITY SAFETY

- Garda Síochána
- Fire brigade

25

FIRST AID IN THE HOME

Minor accidents can generally be attended to in the home. If a more serious accident happens, do not move the person. Cover the patient with a blanket and send for help immediately. Remain calm until help arrives and talk quietly to the patient. Do not give them anything to eat or drink.

THE FIRST-AID KIT

A first-aid kit should contain a selection of items which would help cope with minor accidents in the home. Generally, the kitchen is the best location for the first-aid kit.

The contents of a well stocked first-aid kit should be:

- First-aid book
- Adhesive plasters
- Antiseptic cream
- Bandages (selection)
- Burn spray
- Cotton buds
- Cotton wool
- Cotton gauze (sterile)
- Disinfectant
- Safety pins
- Scissors
- Thermometer
- Tweezers

Medicines should be kept locked in a cupboard, out of the reach of children.

RULES FOR SIMPLE FIRST AID

BURNS

The type and severity of the burn will determine the treatment that should be given. Serious burns require medical attention.

In the case of minor burns (from dry heat) and scalds (from moist heat), place the injured limb in cold water (this excludes air). Do not burst blisters or cover the burn with fat or ointment. Do not handle the area with your fingers. Gently dab dry and cover the area with a sterile dressing. Do not use adhesive plasters. Treat the person for shock.

If a person catches fire, push them to the ground and wrap them in a blanket or coat. Roll them over to put out the fire. If the burns are extensive, send for an ambulance. Calmly explain the extent of the burns. Do not remove burnt clothes that may be attached to the patient's skin. Wait with the patient until help arrives.

CHOKING

When the airways get blocked, a person begins to choke. If the obstruction is not removed very quickly the person could die. Coughing might remove the object.

- In the case of a child, place them, with their face down, over your knee, supporting the chest, and slap between the shoulder blades.
- In the case of an adult, bend the person over and slap them on the back.
- In a more serious case of an adult choking, use the Heimlich manoeuvre. Repeat this if the object is not released. Do not exert too much pressure.

CUTS

Serious cuts and wounds require medical attention. Put a clean cloth over the cut and press firmly to stop bleeding. Take the person to the hospital or doctor. Cuts resulting from rusty metals and animal bites should be treated by the doctor. An anti-tetanus injection may be required.

Minor cuts and grazes:

- Lay the person down. Raise the bleeding limb above the body.
- Immediately control the bleeding by pressing on the cut or wound using a sterile dressing or a clean handkerchief. The bleeding will stop. Do not remove the dressing until the bleeding stops.
- When the bleeding has stopped, wash the wound gently. Dab dry and cover with a fresh sterile dressing or plaster.

FALLS

Do not attempt to move the injured person.

- If they are unable to move send for an ambulance, as bones could be broken or fractured. Cover the person with a blanket to keep them warm until help arrives.
- If the fall is not serious (e.g. resulting in a sprain), apply a cold compress. Go to the doctor if the pain does not ease.

POISONING

Go to the hospital immediately. If possible bring with you the container from which the poisonous substance was taken.

- If the patient is conscious and vomits, bring a sample of this also. Give the patient a drink of milk. This will help to neutralise the poison.
- Call an ambulance if the patient is unconscious and place the patient in the recovery position. Wait calmly until help arrives. Talk to the patient.

26

TECHNOLOGY IN THE HOME

WHAT IS TECHNOLOGY?

In the home, technology is the application of science through appliances and new inventions to make work easier, faster and efficient.

Household tasks which can be done using machines are washing and drying clothes, washing dishes, cleaning carpets, preparing and cooking food.

ADVANTAGES AND DISADVANTAGES OF TECHNOLOGY

ADVANTAGES	DISADVANTAGES
Work is easier	Initial cost can be high
Saves time	Machines can be expensive to run
In-built safety features	Energy consumed could be high
Energy-saving features	Space needed for appliances
More time for other activities	Machines cannot be left unattended

LABOUR-SAVING FOOD PREPARATION MACHINES

- Liquidiser
- Food processor
- Food mixer

ENERGY-SAVING TECHNOLOGY

Appliances in the home which make use of energy-saving technology include cookers, microwave ovens, fridges, dishwashers, washing machines, sewing machines and computers.

27

THE FRIDGE

Fridges are used to keep perishable foods fresh and make them last longer. The low temperatures (2°C to 5°C) slow down the action of enzymes and micro-organisms which cause the food to decay. It is too cold for them to be active.

Having a fridge reduces the number of visits to the shops during the week. Fresh and leftover foods can be stored satisfactorily in the fridge. Fridges reduce food wastage.

HOW THE FRIDGE WORKS

A special liquid (refrigerant) absorbs the heat from the food and air in the fridge and keeps the temperature low. The refrigerant evaporates and circulates through special coils. It recirculates continuously, keeping the inside of the fridge at the correct temperature.

GENERAL GUIDELINES FOR CHOOSING AND BUYING A FRIDGE

1   Research the types of fridge on the market
2   Consider the:
    ● money available
    ● location available in the kitchen
    ● guarantee
    ● size of the family
    ● special features
      (defrosting, star markings, etc.)
3   Delivery arrangements
4   Aftersales service

MODERN FEATURES IN FRIDGES

● Freezer box
● Cold drinks dispenser
● Automatic defrosting
● Varied shelving and door storage arrangements
● Star marking on freezer box

STAR MARKINGS

	Star	Time	Temperature
✳	One star	One week	–6°C
✳✳	Two stars	One month	–12°C
✳✳✳	Three stars	Three months	–18°C
✳✳✳✳	Four stars	Up to one year	–18°C to –25°C (for a freezer)

GUIDELINES FOR USING THE FRIDGE

1   Position fridge away from cooker and radiators
2   Cover all food before putting it in the fridge (this prevents drying out and other foods absorbing strong flavours)
3   Do not place foods too closely together (air must circulate around foods in the fridge)

4 Store food on different shelves and racks according to food type:
  - Meat, poultry and fish near the icebox
  - Milk and eggs in the door
  - Vegetables at the base
5 Do not store apples, bananas, root vegetables or onions in the fridge
6 Allow hot foods to get cold before putting them in the fridge

ROUTINE FOR CLEANING THE FRIDGE

1 Defrost regularly (automatic, semi-automatic, manual)
2 Allow ice to melt naturally
3 Unplug before cleaning
4 Remove all food and wrap to prevent it becoming warm
5 Wash the inside using bread soda and warm water
6 Dry with a clean cloth
7 Wash and dry shelves and removable drawers
8 Wash and polish the outside of the fridge
9 Replace shelves, drawers and food
10 Plug in and switch on

When not in use, unplug the fridge and leave the door ajar to allow the air to circulate.

THE FRIDGE

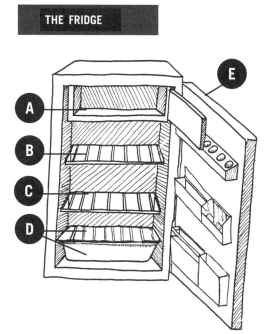

POSITION OF FOOD IN A FRIDGE

PART OF FRIDGE	TEMPERATURE	FOOD
A Freezer box	Coldest part	Frozen foods
B Top shelf	Very cold	Fish, meat, poultry
C Middle shelf	Fairly cold	Leftovers, bacon, rashers, sausages
D Lower shelf/ salad drawer	Least cold	Fruit, salads, vegetables
E Door	Least cold	Butter, cheese, eggs, milk

28

THE COOKER

TYPES OF COOKER

- Free-standing slot-in cooker that fits between units
- Split-level cooker with the hob set into the unit work surface and the oven built-in at eye level
- Range style for larger kitchens

ENERGY/FUEL

The energy used to run cookers includes gas, electricity, solid fuel and oil.

STRUCTURE

Most cookers have:
- Grill (under the hob, at eye level, or in the oven)
- Hob (four burners/rings)
- Oven/double oven (with or without grill)

GAS COOKER

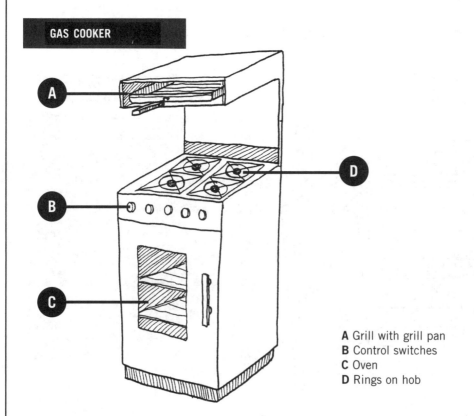

A Grill with grill pan
B Control switches
C Oven
D Rings on hob

CHOOSING AND BUYING A COOKER

POINTS TO CONSIDER

- Money available
- Space and location in the kitchen
- The type of energy supply available
- Guarantee
- Type of cooker (free-standing, split level)
- Modern features and their advantages
- Delivery arrangements

MODERN FEATURES AND THEIR ADVANTAGES

MODERN FEATURES	ADVANTAGES
Autotimers	Oven will automatically turn on and off
Ceramic hob	Easy-care surface
Coloured surfaces	Can match kitchen
Dual elements on grills/hotplates	Saves energy
Fan ovens	Oven has even temperature, food cooks more quickly
Halogen hob	Food begins to cook as soon as the hob is switched on
Hob lid	Hides the hob when not in use
	Keeps the hob clean
	Is an extra work surface
Self-cleaning ovens	Saves labour
Simmerstat on hotplates	Prevents saucepans overflowing

GENERAL GUIDELINES FOR CARE AND CLEANING OF THE COOKER

1 Turn off power supply to the cooker before cleaning
2 Wipe hob and oven surfaces after use
3 Wash and rinse grill pan after each time it is used
4 Clean up spills as soon as they occur
5 Clean ceramic hobs with the recommended cleaner
6 Do not pull saucepans across ceramic hobs, as this will damage the surface
7 Remove shelving from oven and wash in warm soapy water
8 Wash out oven with special oven cleaner if the oven is very dirty (always wear gloves when using a caustic cleaner and protect your clothing and surrounding surfaces); rinse and dry all surfaces carefully
9 Wash and dry the outside surface of the cooker; polish fittings with a soft cloth

29

THE MICROWAVE OVEN

A MICROWAVE OVEN

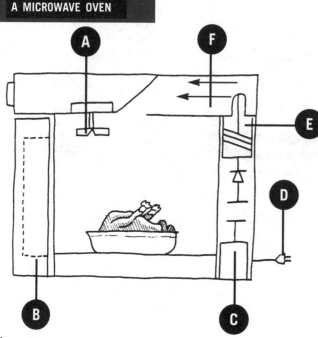

A Stirrer
B Door with safety
  catch
C Transformer
D Plug
E Magnetron
F Wave guide

Advantages:
- Ideal for busy households
- Begins to cook the food immediately
- Cooks food quickly
- Less shrinkage and wastage in food
- Food retains its colour and nutrients
- An economical method of cooking
- Does not produce steam or cooking smells
- Food can be cooked and served in the same dish
- Less washing up (saves labour and time)

Disadvantages:
- Food does not brown unless a browning dish or a combination microwave oven is used
- Some foods cannot be cooked in a microwave oven
- Special dishes must be used (metal dishes or tins must not be used)
- Standing time must be added to the cooking time

RULES FOR USING A MICROWAVE OVEN

Note: Always follow the manufacturer's instructions.

1   Do not operate when empty
2   Do not use metal in the microwave oven
3   Allow extra time for larger quantities
4   Use special microwave covers on dishes or cover with microwave oven film. Prick the surface of the film before putting the dish in the oven. Prick any food with a skin before cooking
5   Allow standing time when food is removed
6   Clean up spills immediately
7   Do not use if the door is faulty

WORK ROUTINE FOR CLEANING THE MICROWAVE OVEN

Note: Check the manufacturer's instructions.

1   Turn off the power supply
2   Remove turntable and wash, rinse and dry
3   Wash the door and inside with warm soapy water; rinse and dry
4   Replace turntable
5   Wipe and polish the outside of the microwave oven

30

SMALL APPLIANCES

Advantages of small appliances:

- Labour saving
- Save time
- Inexpensive to buy
- Do not require a lot of storage space

- Help speed up food preparation techniques (shredding, blending, chopping, grating)

TYPES OF APPLIANCE

Some small appliances use a small motor to do the work. Others use thermostats to control heat.

APPLIANCES WITH A MOTOR

Blender or liquidiser   Electric carving knife
Food processor   Electric can opener
Food mixer (large/small)

APPLIANCES WITH A THERMOSTAT

Deep-fat fryer   Slow cooker
Kettle   Toaster
Sandwich maker

CHOOSING AND BUYING SMALL APPLIANCES

POINTS TO CONSIDER

- How much money is available?
- Will the appliance be used frequently?
- Is the appliance the right size or capacity?
- What is the appliance made from?
- How many tasks can the appliance perform?
- How efficiently does it perform these tasks?
- Is it easy and safe to use?
- Is it easy to clean?
- Does it have a guarantee?

GENERAL GUIDELINES FOR USING SMALL APPLIANCES

1   Read the manufacturer's leaflet before using the appliance

2   Follow the manufacturer's instructions carefully
3   Follow all safety guidelines
4   Use with care, especially appliances with sharp blades
5   Do not overfill blenders, liquidisers and food processors with hot liquids (e.g. soups)
6   Use the recommended quantities
7   Choose soft margarine for food processors
8   Use the correct attachments for the task in hand
9   Select the recommended speed on all appliances

ROUTINE FOR CLEANING SMALL APPLIANCES

1   Follow the manufacturer's instructions
2   Take appliances apart carefully (blades, bowls, etc.)
3   Never put parts containing motors or thermostats into water
4   Wipe with a cloth rinsed out in warm soapy water
5   Wash, rinse and dry blades, bowls and other attachments as indicated in the instruction booklet
6   Do not put lids into place (allow the air to circulate so that the appliances do not develop a stale smell)

31

SERVICES IN THE HOME

IMPORTANT SERVICES SUPPLIED TO THE HOME

- Electricity
- Gas
- Water
- Water disposal
- Television
- Telephone
- Sewage and bin collection

ELECTRICITY

Wind power, hydroelectric power and fuels (turf, oil, gas, coal) are used to generate electricity.

A service cable attached to the fuse box in the home brings electricity from the generating station to the home. Electricity is carried around the house to the various points by wires.

MEASURING ELECTRICAL CONSUMPTION

Electrical consumption is measured in units (kilowatt-hour). Consumption is recorded by a meter in the home.

ELECTRICAL WIRES

The three wires found in an electrical appliance are:

EARTH • LIVE • NEUTRAL

The earth wire acts as a safety device should a fault occur.
The live wire brings electricity to the appliance.
The neutral wire carries the current back to the generator.

WIRING COLOUR CODE FOR PLUGS

Earth   Green/yellow
Live   Brown
Neutral   Blue

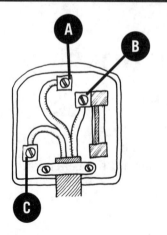

DIAGRAM OF A PLUG

A Earth B Live C Neutral

Rules for wiring a plug:
1 Unplug the appliance
2 Loosen all screws and put the wires into position
3 Make sure that the plug has a cord grip
4 Tighten the screws into place

Safety symbol: 'Doubly insulated', with two square boxes, one inside the other (refer to section on Consumer Education).

WHAT IS A FUSE?

A fuse is a weak link which melts when a fault occurs. This breaks the circuit and stops the electrical current. Fuses are found in appliances and in the fuse box.

Causes of blown fuses:

- Overloaded circuits
- Live wires touching neutral wires
- Faulty thermostats in appliances

WHAT IS A RESIDUAL CURRENT DEVICE?

This is a safety device found in immersion heaters and electric showers.

LIGHTING IN THE HOME

Good lighting is important for safety and comfort in the home. Sources of light are natural sunlight and artificial light.

Natural light: The main source of natural sunlight is through windows and glass doors. The aspect of the room and the position of the windows will influence the quality of the natural light.

Artificial light: Filament bulbs, fluorescent bulbs and strips and compact fluorescent lights are sources of artificial lighting. The function of the room will influence the type and strength of the artificial lighting chosen.

CFLs: The compact fluorescent light (CFL) is the latest energy-efficient artificial lighting system available. At present each CFL bulb is expensive, but it will last longer than ordinary bulbs. The shape of CFLs is rather unattractive.

LIGHTING ARRANGEMENTS IN THE HOME

ROOM	SUGGESTED LIGHT FITTING
Kitchen	Fluorescent strips under units
	Central fluorescent or spot lights
Living-room	Table lamps
	Wall lights
	Central light
	Standard lamp
Bedroom	Table lamps
	Wall lights over the bed
	Spots angled to light up the inside of wardrobes
Hall/landings	Central light fittings which light up both areas and the steps of the stairs
Bathroom	Central light
	Fluorescent strip over washhand basin

Importance of good lighting:
- Prevents eyestrain when reading, studying or sewing
- Allows us to see everything we do (washing, cooking, etc.)
- Prevents accidents (on stairs, when using kitchen knives, etc.)

Guidelines for good lighting:
- Good lighting will not produce glare, shadows or flickering
- Choose good-quality fittings with suitable shades
- Buy fittings and shades that are safe
- Always use shades over bulbs and fluorescent tubes
- Light up stairs and steps
- For detailed work (studying, reading) use strong direct light

Replacing a bulb:
Turn off the switch. Allow bulbs that have blown to cool down. Remove the blown bulb and dispose of it safely. Insert a new bulb and check that it is secure. Turn on switch to check that it is working.

GAS

Piped gas is available in cities and some large towns. It is a quick and efficient form of energy. Bottled gas is used where piped gas is unavailable. As gas is a non-renewable energy source, use it economically.

TYPES OF GAS AVAILABLE

Natural gas: A service pipe brings the gas into each house for cooking and heating. A meter records the amount used. A valve is located at the point of entry. The gas can be turned off if there is a leak or during servicing of the system. Gas consumption is measured in cubic meters.

Bottled gas: This is used for heating and cooking in houses, caravans, mobile homes and when camping. Local shops stock bottled gas.

IMPORTANT SAFETY GUIDELINES FOR GAS

- Buy gas appliances which carry a recognised safety label
- Qualified people should install gas appliances and heating systems
- Service systems and appliances regularly
- Use gas appliances in well-ventilated rooms

- If you smell gas in your home, take action immediately

What to do when there is a gas leak:
- Act immediately
- Do not light a match or a cigarette or turn on a light switch
- Open all windows and doors to allow the gas to escape
- Turn off the gas supply at the point of entry
- Send for the gas company

WATER

A clean, pure water supply is an essential service to homes.

SOME USES OF WATER IN THE HOME

- Washing
- Cleaning
- Cooking
- Drinking
- Preparing food

Local authorities are responsible for supplying water to the homes in their area. From the reservoirs water is sent into the home through the mains. A storage tank in the home holds a supply of water for immediate use. Wells supply water to some homes in country areas.

WHAT IS HARD WATER?

Water that contains dissolved minerals which make it difficult to form a lather is called hard water. Hard water forms limescale which builds up in kettles and pipes.

WATER TREATMENT

- To remove harmful solid substances, water is treated using a filtering process.
- To destroy harmful bacteria, chlorine is added to the water.
- To prevent tooth decay and strengthen teeth, fluoride is added.

BLOCKED SINKS – WHAT TO DO

The plunger:
- Remove any food from the sink.
- Half-fill the sink with water.

- Put the plunger over the plug hole.
- Push down and release until the blockage is cleared.

Washing soda:
- Using boiling water, dissolve washing soda through the plug hole into the waste pipe.

U-bends:
- If the above methods fail, put a basin under the U-bend.
- Unscrew the pipe at the U-bend under the sink.
- Remove the blockage.
- Rinse out the U-bend pipe with hot water and put back into position.

FROZEN PIPES – WHAT TO DO

- Turn off the water coming into the house.
- Wrap the pipes with towels dipped in hot water.
- Use a hairdryer on a low setting to thaw out the pipes. Work from the taps back along the pipes.

BURST PIPES – WHAT TO DO

- Turn off water coming into the house at the mains under the sink.
- Turn on all cold-water taps to empty the water system.
- Switch off the central heating system.
- If a solid fuel cooker or a stove with a backboiler is linked into the central heating system, allow it to go out. Do not refuel.
- Send for the plumber immediately.

HEATING IN THE HOME

An efficient heating system is essential to make the home energy efficient and save money. The fuels used to run central heating systems are oil, gas and solid fuel (open fires and solid-fuel cookers). The gas can be off the mains or from a supply tank in the garden. Oil is stored in a large tank outside the house and piped into a boiler.

FACTORS WHICH INFLUENCE CHOICE OF HEATING SYSTEM

- Effectiveness, energy efficiency and safety of the system
- Money available

- Lifestyle
- Size of house
- Location of house

HEAT TRANSFER

Heat is transferred in the home in three ways, convection, conduction and radiation (for more information see Cooking Methods).

METHODS OF HEATING THE HOME

- Central heating is a system which radiates heat from a central source and circulates it around the house through pipes and radiators. Full central heating provides heat for the whole house.
- Partial central heating gives background heating and may only heat some areas of a house.
- Spot heating is provided by electric or gas heating appliances and open fires.

32

THE COMMUNITY

WHAT IS AN AMENITY?

An amenity can be described as an attractive feature in a local area which can be enjoyed by those who live there (river walk, park, gardens, playground, banks, shops, sports centres and beaches).

WHAT IS A COMMUNITY?

A group of people who live in the same area are collectively called a community.

WHAT ARE COMMUNITY RESOURCES?

These are services available, such as schools, library, community centre, hospital, post office. The people who live in the area are also a community resource, because they bring with them knowledge and skills.

SERVICES

STATUTORY SERVICES

- Health board
- Local authority housing
- Post office
- Social welfare services
- Services such as water, electricity

VOLUNTARY SERVICES

- Community Alert
- Heritage associations
- Residents associations
- The Samaritans

OTHER ORGANISATIONS

- Earthwatch
- GAA
- Greenpeace
- Hospice Movement
- ISPCC
- Neighbourhood Watch
- Rehabilitation Institute
- St Vincent de Paul

33

ENERGY-FRIENDLY HOMES

Saving energy in the home is very important if we are to use the resources available efficiently. Using less energy saves money and protects the environment.

WAYS OF SAVING ENERGY: GENERAL GUIDELINES

AREA	SUGGESTIONS
Electricity	Make full use of the oven (cook several dishes together)
	Keep appliances serviced and in good working order
	Buy appliances which have energy-saving features
	Take showers instead of baths

	Use a pressure cooker to cook complete meals
Lighting	Switch off lights when not needed
	Use CFL bulbs for internal and external lighting
Central heating	Turn down thermostats
	Turn off radiators in rooms when not in use
	Close curtains to prevent heat escaping
Water heating	Lag the cylinder
	Put timer on immersion heater
	Use 'Nightsaver' electricity

INSULATING THE HOME

AREA	SUGGESTIONS
Attic	Fibre-glass blanket
	Loose-fill insulating material
Cylinder	Lagging jacket
Floors	Underlay fitted correctly
	Fitted carpets
Walls	Cavity walls
	Foam or polystyrene insulation
Windows/doors	Double glazing
	Heavy lined curtains
	Draught excluders (metal, plastic, foam)

34

ENVIRONMENTAL ISSUES

The quality of our lives is influenced by the products we use and how they affect the environment around us. Air and water are frequently damaged by pollution.

POLLUTION PROBLEMS

WHERE	CAUSES
Air	Toxic chemical fumes from factories and industry
	Lead in petrol
	Fumes from cars, buses, lorries
	Aerosols and fridges releasing CFCs
Water	Organic waste (slurry, sewage)
	Dead animals
	Rubbish
	Toxic chemical waste from industry
	Excess fertiliser seeping from land
	Phosphates
Noise	Constant traffic
	Loud music/radios/television
Others	Plastic bags
	Rubbish and litter (paper, plastic containers)
	Old cars
	Old equipment (fridges, washing machines, etc.)

THE OZONE LAYER

The ozone layer is a layer of the upper atmosphere which protects us against ultraviolet rays from the sun. CFCs (chlorofluorocarbons) and halons disrupt the ozone layer by causing it to become thinner and allowing the ultraviolet rays through the atmosphere. This results in an increased risk of skin cancer, eye disorders and damage to plant life.

ENVIRONMENTAL GUIDELINES

- Avoid aerosols which contain CFCs
- Buy alternatives to aerosol products (ozone-friendly)
- Choose refill type products
- Choose products in biodegradable packaging
- Choose energy-efficient equipment
- Use CFL bulbs
- Develop a recycling plan for the home
- Avoid detergents with phosphates
- Dispose of old fridges properly
- Limit use of consumer goods
- Avoid waste

WASTE DISPOSAL

Waste must be disposed of safely and hygienically to avoid health hazards. Local authorities collect waste in cities and some towns. In a number of country towns and rural areas, private companies collect waste from households for a fee.

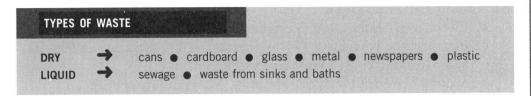

TYPES OF WASTE

| DRY | ➔ | cans ● cardboard ● glass ● metal ● newspapers ● plastic |
| LIQUID | ➔ | sewage ● waste from sinks and baths |

ORGANIC HOUSEHOLD WASTE

Waste can also be classified as inorganic or organic.

Waste from baths, showers, sinks and toilets is removed from the house through pipes which are linked to a sewage treatment plant or a septic tank.

The waste is broken down by bacteria into harmless substances. These substances are released into the sea, lake or river. Raw untreated sewage, by law, cannot be pumped into the sea, lakes or rivers.

Septic tanks are emptied and their contents removed for treatment.

BINS

Bins are used to hold waste in kitchens and outside the house. Keep bins covered at all times. Weekly bin collections are a feature of many cities, towns and country areas.

Pedal bins: Pedal bins are best for kitchens, provided they are lined, emptied and washed out daily.

Dustbins: Large dustbins can be of plastic or metal. Wrap all waste products before transferring them into the outdoor bin. Keep bins covered at all times, away from the house, and clean regularly. Wash out with hot soapy water, disinfect and dry thoroughly.

RECYCLING

The human race produces millions of tons of organic and inorganic waste each year. Recycling systems dispose of waste products in an environmentally friendly way if they are planned correctly. There are many ways in which the home can be organised to dispose of waste in a manner which would not damage the environment.

RECYCLING IN THE HOME

- Glass, paper, metal and oils can be returned to collection banks located around the country. Some collection banks can be found in supermarket car parks.
- Clothes can be delivered to a clothes bank or a charity shop. If there is time and you have the skills, you could consider recycling clothes at home (making clothes for younger children).
- Natural materials (vegetable peelings, grass cuttings, papers and wood cuttings) can be added to the compost heap in the garden.

35

THE FAMILY

WHAT IS A FAMILY?

A family is a group of people closely related by blood or by marriage. They may share the same name and in some cases live in the same house. Families can be made up of adults, teenagers, elderly people, toddlers and babies.

People can be parents, siblings, grandparents, cousins, aunts and uncles. A family unit is generally a smaller group of these people.

TYPES OF FAMILY		
NUCLEAR	**EXTENDED**	**SINGLE-PARENT**
Parents	Grandparents	Parent
Children	Aunts	Children
	Uncles	
	Cousins	

DIFFERENCES BETWEEN TYPES OF FAMILY

- Members of the nuclear family live in the same house.
- In the extended family, members live very close or in the same house.
- Single-parent families have one parent and children. Parents may live on their own with children because they are divorced, separated, unmarried or widowed.

FUNCTIONS OF A FAMILY

The family satisfies the basic needs of the individuals in the family. People have emotional and physical needs.

Emotional needs	**Physical needs**
Love	Clothing
Relationships with others	Food
Security	Shelter and protection

The needs of each individual are fulfilled, depending on the cultural, economic and social resources available within the family. Each person within a family has responsibilities and roles to fulfil.

FACTORS INFLUENCING FAMILY LIFE		
CULTURAL	**ECONOMIC**	**SOCIAL**
Race	Salary	Education
Religion	Social benefits	Lifestyle
Language	Employment	Employment

ROLES WITHIN THE FAMILY

WHAT IS A ROLE?

A role can be defined as the right way to behave within the family (acceptable appropriate behaviour).

CHILDREN

Children have few responsibilities. They may be asked to help set the table, make their beds and help with small tasks. Childhood is generally a time free of responsibilities, allowing time for play. Parents expect children to behave well, be polite and do as they are told (go to bed, etc.).

ADOLESCENTS

Adolescents are expected to take on more responsibilities (household chores, looking after smaller siblings). As adolescents move from childhood dependence towards adulthood there are many physical and emotional changes taking place. Teenagers try to make parents aware of these changes, as they learn to become more independent. This sometimes causes conflict.

PARENTS

Parents have a very responsible role in the family. They must:
- Set a good example for their children
- Provide for the emotional and physical needs of their children
- Create a happy home environment
- Teach their children right from wrong
- Listen to their children
- Provide advice and guidance
- Be supportive of each other

RELATIONSHIPS

The word 'relationship' describes how we get on with others. Relationships are influenced by the role adopted.

Types of relationship within a family:
- Husband and wife
- Parents and children
- Siblings
- Grandparents and grandchildren
- Grandparents and their own children

The key to good relationships is good communication.

36

ADOLESCENCE

Adolescence is a time of considerable change and development. As teenagers move from childhood to adulthood, they experience physical, emotional, social and moral changes. Their roles and relationships are developing and changing and this can be a happy or an unhappy experience. Adolescents enjoy having greater independence from their parents.

PHYSICAL CHANGES

Puberty begins at different times for different individuals. Hormones are responsible for the physical changes which take place during adolescence. Some physical changes include:
- Very rapid growth, increase in height and weight
- Growth of body hair; facial hair on boys, underarm and pubic hair on boys and girls
- Girls develop breasts
- Girls start menstruation
- Boys may experience erections and ejaculations

EMOTIONAL CHANGES

Relationships develop and are taken very seriously. Adolescents can experience confusion and suffer pain if relationships do not work out. Adolescents begin to understand what is involved in developing a mature relationship.

MENTAL CHANGES

Mental development during adolescence involves the teenager beginning to think and question in a more adult way. Teenagers also begin to examine the world in which they live and to think about their future.

MORAL AND SOCIAL DEVELOPMENT

Adolescents begin to examine the attitudes, behaviour and ideas around them. They try to find a set of values that have meaning for them. Their moral and social values will be influenced by their relationship with parents and family and their peer group. Their search for a personal identity will eventually lead to greater self-esteem and self-confidence.

INFLUENCES ON THE ADOLESCENT

Adolescents are influenced by:
- Parents
- Environment
- School
- Family
- Peer group
- Community
- Media

GENDER

WHAT IS GENDER?

Gender is defined as the state of being male or female.

WHAT IS A GENDER ROLE?

This defines separate roles for males and females. There is no exchange of roles. Gender roles are learned in the home and outside the home.

GENDER EQUITY

This involves treating males and females equally, at home, in school, at work and in the community.

Gender equity enables males and females to:
- Choose the same careers
- Share household tasks

- Develop skills, free from stereotyping
- Decide to stay at home to bring up their children
- Express their emotions
- Develop self-esteem and self-confidence

PERSONAL DEVELOPMENT

WHAT ARE NORMS?

A norm is the acceptable appropriate behaviour for living in society. Most people behave responsibly. Some people are irresponsible.

Examples of norms:
- Respecting parents and other people
- Being polite (thanking people)
- Attending school regularly
- Being a good citizen
- Being on time
- Helping others

Examples of irresponsible behaviour:
- Throwing litter on the street
- Shouting on the street
- Drinking to excess
- Putting your feet on the table
- Not going to school
- Being rude to others
- Taking drugs

PERSONAL SKILLS

Personal skills enable us to work with others. It helps if we can listen carefully, speak clearly and logically, be co-operative, be pleasant and look at the other person. If a problem occurs, it helps to use negotiation skills and to listen. Listening and negotiation are important when dealing with conflict situations.

LEISURE

Adolescents should make use of their free time, away from their studies, to relax. Leisure provides adolescents with the opportunity to refresh themselves so that they are better able to cope with the demands of studying and attending school. Some leisure activities are expensive, others cost nothing.

LEISURE ACTIVITIES

Reading, chess, cinema, music, dance, classes (learn a new language or sport, etc.), computers, sports activities, painting, voluntary work, visiting friends or relatives, visiting museums and heritage sites, needlecraft, gardening.

Choose an activity that is enjoyable for you and which can fit into your lifestyle. It should also be affordable.

37

GOOD HEALTH

Good health is essential for people to enjoy a good quality of life. Health can be examined under emotional, mental, physical, spiritual and social well-being. Each of us is responsible for looking after our own health. The more vulnerable people in society will need others to look after them.

CHARACTERISTICS OF A HEALTHY LIFESTYLE

A healthy lifestyle depends on:
- Healthy, balanced diet
- Rest
- Exercise
- Good personal hygiene
- Good home hygiene
- Healthy attitude to life

MENTAL HEALTH

Mental health influences how we feel and how we behave towards ourselves and others. Good mental health involves a positive state of mind and a positive attitude to life. People with good mental health are able to like themselves, get on with others and cope with difficulties when they arise. People with poor mental health find it difficult to cope on a day-to-day basis with themselves, with others and with problems.

It is natural for all of us to feel at times that we cannot cope. When this happens we depend on the support of family and friends.

FACTORS INFLUENCING GOOD MENTAL HEALTH

- Confidence
- Physical health

- Experiences in life
- Family relationships
- Attitude to life
  (being pessimistic or optimistic)

- Relationships with others
  outside the family
- Social environment
  (home and community)

EMOTIONS

Our emotions influence our state of mental health. Basic emotions include anger, fear and love.

STRESS

Stress is the feeling of tension we get when we feel we are not coping with the demands being made on us.

STRESS-RELATED PROBLEMS

Problems associated with severe stress include anxiety, breathing problems, bowel problems, heart problems and ulcers.

WAYS TO AVOID STRESS

- Enjoy life each day
- Develop a positive attitude to life
- Develop strategies to cope with problems
- Talk with someone about the difficulties you are experiencing
- Ask for help and advice
- Eat a healthy diet
- Take time over meals and relax while eating
- Take some form of exercise daily
- Go for a walk in the fresh air
- Relax after work
- Get a good night's rest

GOOD PHYSICAL HEALTH

To maintain good physical health it is essential to:
- Eat a healthy, balanced diet
- Get an average of eight hours sleep each night

- Have a good personal hygiene routine
- Have regular health check-ups
- Take regular exercise in the open air when possible

38

THE SKIN

STRUCTURE OF THE SKIN

Skin covers the whole body. The skin is made up of two layers, the epidermis and the dermis.

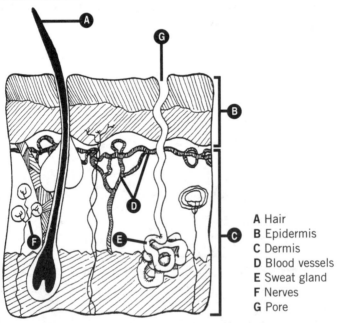

A Hair
B Epidermis
C Dermis
D Blood vessels
E Sweat gland
F Nerves
G Pore

THE EPIDERMIS

This is the outer layer of the skin, consisting of dead cells which are constantly wearing away and being replaced.

THE DERMIS

This is the name of the inner layer of the skin. It has a complex structure. The dermis is made up of:
- Blood vessels (which bring nutrients to the cells and remove waste)
- Fat cells (which insulate the body and act as an energy store)
- Hair follicles and roots
- Muscles
- Nerves (which enable us to feel cold, heat and sensations)
- Oil glands (which produce oil to keep hair and skin lubricated)
- Sweat glands (which remove waste through the pores)

FUNCTIONS OF THE SKIN

- Acts as an insulator and energy reserve
- Enables us to feel sensations
- Manufacture of vitamin D when exposed to the sun
- Prevents the loss of body fluids
- Protects the body against disease
- Outer layer of the skin protects the dermis
- Regulates body temperature
- Removes excess water and waste products

Note: Body temperature is 37°C.
The body releases about 1 litre of sweat per day.

SKIN CARE

Body odour (BO) is produced by bacteria on the skin. A good daily hygiene routine will prevent BO.

DAILY HYGIENE ROUTINE

A good daily hygiene routine is essential for good health. Sweat and oil glands are very active during adolescence. To feel fresh each day:
- Shower to remove sweat, bacteria and dead cells using warm water
- Shower after sporting activities and change into fresh clothes
- Use deodorants or antiperspirants
- Change into clean clothes, especially underwear, every day
- Wash hands frequently, especially after using the toilet
- Wash hands before handling food

CARING FOR THE SKIN

- Eat a balanced diet
- Drink plenty of water every day
- Take plenty of fresh air and exercise
- Get enough sleep
- Avoid alcohol and cigarettes
- Avoid over-exposure to the sun (use high-protection sunscreens)

ACNE

Acne is a skin complaint resulting from overactive oil glands and blocked pores. It occurs during adolescence. Bacteria can become lodged in the pores and cause pimples or blackheads.

Acne can be controlled by:

- Establishing a skin-care routine
- Washing the skin with a medicated soap
- Drinking lots of water
- Eating fresh fruit and vegetables
- Avoiding greasy foods

CARING FOR YOURSELF

HAND CARE

Wash hands frequently during the day. Dry hands carefully after washing. Use a hand cream to prevent chapping and dryness. Manicure regularly. Use gloves when doing dirty jobs (cleaning out the fire, gardening).

FEET CARE

Choose well-fitting shoes. Change tights or socks each day. Wash feet daily and dry well. Pay attention to the area between the toes.

Problems associated with feet include corns, bunions, verrucae and athlete's foot.

HAIR CARE

Brush hair each day to remove tangles. Wash hair at least once a week. If hair is greasy it might be necessary to wash it every three days. Rinse well, condition, comb and towel dry. Avoid using the hair dryer every time. Avoid bleaching and colouring hair too often.

Keep brushes and combs clean. Wash them frequently. Do not lend your brushes or combs to other people, as dandruff and head lice can be passed on.

SOME HYGIENE AND CARE PRODUCTS

- Antiperspirant
- Cleanser, toner and moisturiser
- Deodorant
- Hand cream
- Soap
- Shampoo and conditioner
- Toothpaste

39

THE TEETH

TYPES OF TEETH

TEETH	FUNCTION
Incisors	Biting, cutting and grinding food
Canines	Tearing food
Pre-molars	Crushing and grinding food
Molars	Crushing and grinding food

HOW MANY TEETH?

Children have 20 teeth and adults on average have 32 teeth.

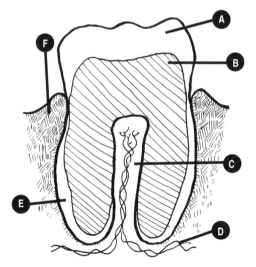

STRUCTURE OF THE TOOTH

The tooth is made up of the crown, the neck and the root.
- The crown is the part of the tooth visible above the gum.
- The neck is the part between the crown and the root.
- The root is hidden in the gum.

A Enamel **D** Blood supply and nerves
B Dentine **E** Cementum
C Pulp **F** Gum

ENAMEL

Enamel, the outer covering of the tooth, is the hardest substance in the body.

DENTINE

The dentine is just inside the enamel. It is not as hard as the enamel.

PULP CAVITY

The pulp cavity is the central part of the tooth. It contains nerves and blood vessels.

CEMENTUM

Cementum covers the root of the tooth.

TEETH PROBLEMS

Bacteria, food and plaque are responsible for tooth decay or dental caries.

WHAT IS PLAQUE?

Plaque is the substance which coats the teeth after a meal or a snack. Plaque sticks to the teeth. It contains bacteria. The bacteria work on the food, forming an acid. This acid then eats into the enamel, causing cavities to form. Gum disease may also result from a build-up of plaque and poor dental hygiene.

WHAT IS PERIODONTAL DISEASE?

This is a dental disease which damages the area surrounding the tooth. The parts affected include the bone, gum and tissues. It is important to have all dental problems treated, as they can affect general health and well-being.

TEETH CARE

- Visit the dentist regularly (every six months)
- Wash teeth regularly – morning, after eating, and last thing at night before going to bed – to prevent plaque forming
- Choose calcium and vitamin D-rich foods (for strong teeth)
- Eat crunchy fruits and vegetables
- Avoid sugary snacks, drinks, biscuits and cakes
- Do not snack between meals

- Do not attempt to use teeth to open bottles or cut thread
- Choose a toothpaste that contains fluoride
- Choose a good quality toothbrush
- Use dental products (dental floss, disclosing tablets, mouthwash, toothbrush, toothpaste)

WHAT IS FLUORIDE?

Fluoride is a mineral which can occur naturally in water. Fluoride is added to drinking water and to toothpaste to strengthen teeth and reduce tooth decay. Local authorities add fluoride directly to the water supply.

40

THE RESPIRATORY SYSTEM

STRUCTURE

A Epiglottis
B Trachea
C Rings of cartilage
D Bronchus
E Bronchioles
F Alveoli
G Right lung

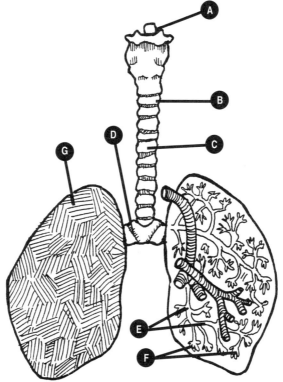

Note: Healthy lungs are pink in colour.

POSITION AND SHAPE OF LUNGS

The two lungs lie above the diaphragm, in the chest cavity. The ribs, sternum (breast bone) and the back bone protect the lungs.

The lungs are like two sponge bags when filled with air. The base (the wider end) rests just above the diaphragm. The pointed end is at the top.

HOW THE LUNGS WORK

- We breathe in through our mouth and nose, where air is warmed and filtered.
- At the back of the throat is the pharynx and the epiglottis. The epiglottis prevents food going down the windpipe or trachea.
- Air passes down through the trachea into the bronchi. There are two bronchi, one entering each lung.
- The trachea is made up of rings of cartilage. The trachea divides into two bronchi.
- From each bronchus, the air passes into the bronchioles and eventually into the alveoli.
- In the alveoli the exchange of gases takes place between the capillaries and the lungs.

EXCHANGE OF GASES

Oxygen passes through the walls of the alveoli into the blood capillaries. Carbon dioxide and water pass through the walls of the blood capillaries into the alveoli. When we breathe out, carbon dioxide and water are expelled from the body in the stale exhaled air.

FUNCTIONS OF THE LUNGS

- To take oxygen from the air
- To remove carbon dioxide from the body

DISEASES OF THE RESPIRATORY SYSTEM

SOME COMMON DISEASES

- Bronchitis
- Cancer (throat, lungs)
- Colds
- Laryngitis
- Pneumonia
- Tuberculosis

GUIDELINES FOR HEALTHY LUNGS

- Do not smoke or stay in a smoky atmosphere for a long time
- Learn to breathe correctly
- Look after colds and bronchitis before they develop into something more serious
- Ventilate the home properly
- Take aerobic exercise to strengthen the respiratory and circulatory systems
- If you suffer from asthma, follow the advice given by your doctor

41

THE CIRCULATORY SYSTEM

The circulatory system brings blood with nutrients and oxygen around the body. It also carries impure blood with waste products away from the cells and brings it to the lungs to be purified.

THE HEART

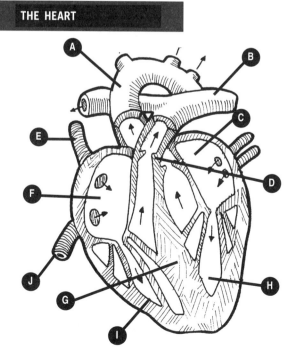

THE HEART

POSITION AND SHAPE OF HEART

The heart is located in the chest cavity between the two lungs, above the diaphragm.

A Aorta
B Pulmonary artery
C Left auricle or atrium
D Semi-lunar valve
E Superior vena cava
F Right auricle or atrium
G Septum
H Left ventricle
I Right ventricle
J Inferior vena cava

The heart is a pear-shaped organ with the pointed end, or apex, turned downwards and the broad end at the top. The heart pumps the blood around the body through blood vessels, arteries, veins and capillaries.

STRUCTURE

The heart is made up of cardiac muscle. It is divided down the centre by a wall (the septum).

There are four chambers in the heart, two on either side of the septum. The top two chambers are called atria. The lower chambers are known as ventricles.

The atria are separated from the ventricles by semi-lunar valves (tricuspid valve on the right, bicuspid valve on the left). The valves prevent blood flowing back into the chambers.

THE PULMONARY CIRCULATION

- Impure blood from the body is emptied by the superior and inferior venae cavae into the right atrium.
- The impure blood passes from the right atrium into the right ventricle through the tricuspid valves.
- The right ventricle contracts and pushes the blood into the pulmonary artery, which brings the impure blood to the lungs.
- In the lungs the blood is purified.
- The purified blood leaves the lungs through the pulmonary vein and returns to the left atrium of the heart.
- The blood is pumped into the left ventricle.
- The left ventricle contracts and pushes the blood into the aorta.
- From the aorta the purified blood is sent around the body.

BLOOD VESSELS

The body contains three types of blood vessels: arteries, veins and capillaries.

ARTERIES

All arteries except one (pulmonary artery) carry oxygenated blood. Artery walls are elastic and thick. Arteries divide into arterioles. Arterioles divide into capillaries.

CAPILLARIES

Capillaries have thin single-cell walls which allow oxygen and nutrients to enter and carbon dioxide to leave body cells.

VEINS

Vein walls are thinner than those of arteries. Veins carry blood towards the heart. The veins carry impure blood, except for the pulmonary veins, which are the exception. Veins have valves to prevent back-flow of blood. Veins divide into venules.

THE BLOOD

On average the adult body has about five litres of blood. The blood is composed of plasma, red and white blood cells and platelets.

PLASMA

Plasma is a yellow-coloured liquid in the blood, in which red and white blood cells and platelets are found.

RED BLOOD CELLS

Red blood cells are composed of haemoglobin, which picks up oxygen in the lungs and carries it around to the cells of the body.

WHITE BLOOD CELLS

White blood cells fight infection by surrounding and killing the bacteria in the blood.

PLATELETS

Platelets help the blood to clot when we receive a cut.

FUNCTIONS OF BLOOD

1. To pick up and transport:
   - oxygen to cells and tissues
   - nutrients around the body to cells and tissues
   - carbon dioxide from cells and to bring the impure blood to the lungs to be purified
   - hormones
2. To fight disease
3. To form clots over cuts
4. To regulate body temperature

42

THE REPRODUCTIVE SYSTEMS

FEMALE REPRODUCTIVE SYSTEM

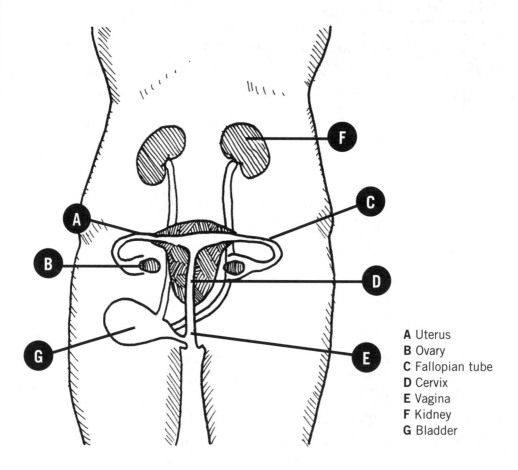

A Uterus
B Ovary
C Fallopian tube
D Cervix
E Vagina
F Kidney
G Bladder

STRUCTURE OF FEMALE REPRODUCTIVE SYSTEM

The ovaries are situated on either side of the lower abdomen. Two sex hormones, progesterone and oestrogen, are produced by the ovaries. The ovaries contain a supply of unripened ova. One of the ovaries releases an ovum once a month. The fallopian tubes link the ovaries to the uterus. The uterus (womb) is a muscular organ which carries the unborn baby during pregnancy. The neck of the uterus is called the cervix. The muscular tube leading from the cervix is called the vagina.

MENSTRUATION

Menstruation lasts from puberty to menopause. The menstrual cycle varies in length but is around 28 days on average. It can vary from month to month, depending on the individual. Each month one of the ovaries releases an ovum, or egg. The egg travels from the ovary through the fallopian tube to the uterus. The wall of the uterus has thickened in preparation for a baby. If conception does not occur, the egg and lining of the womb are expelled from the body during menstruation. This bleeding from the uterus is referred to as a 'period'.

FERTILISATION, IMPLANTATION AND PREGNANCY

During sexual intercourse, the erect penis is placed into the female's vagina. Semen is released into the vagina. Sperm travel through the cervix, the uterus and into the fallopian tubes. If a fertile ovum is present, a sperm may fertilise it. If the ovum is fertilised, the female becomes pregnant.

The fertilised ovum begins to divide into more cells as it moves down the fallopian tubes. This group of cells becomes the embryo and attaches, or implants, itself to the lining of the uterus. The embryo is attached to the placenta by the umbilical cord. The embryo develops into the foetus.

The placenta provides the developing baby with oxygen and food during pregnancy. It acts as a filter between the mother and the developing baby. Amniotic fluid surrounds the baby and protects it during pregnancy.

Pregnancy generally lasts about 40 weeks.

BIRTH

After the waters (amniotic fluid) break, labour begins. During labour the uterus contracts at intervals and the cervix dilates. The contractions become stronger and closer together as the mother is near to giving birth. The cervix widens to allow the baby to be born.

When the baby is born, the umbilical cord is clamped at the navel. After the baby is born, the placenta and the remains of the umbilical cord are expelled (this is referred to as the afterbirth).

MALE REPRODUCTIVE SYSTEM

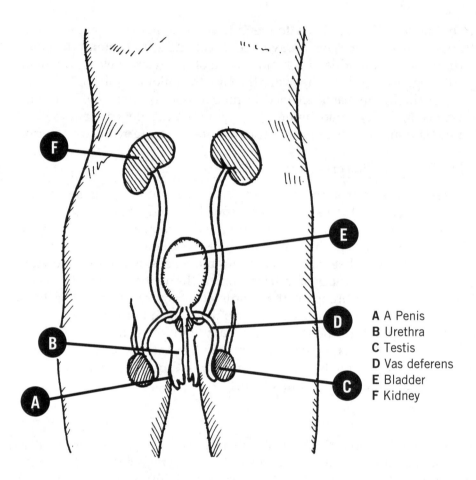

A A Penis
B Urethra
C Testis
D Vas deferens
E Bladder
F Kidney

STRUCTURE AND FUNCTION OF MALE REPRODUCTIVE SYSTEM

In males the testes, which produce sperm from the time of puberty, lie outside the body in a sac called the scrotum. The testes produce the hormone testosterone. They also make sperm.

During sexual intercourse, mature sperm in semen travel from the testes through the vas deferens to the penis. They are released into the female's vagina and from there travel to the fallopian tubes. If a fertile ovum is present, fertilisation may take place and pregnancy will result.

43

HEALTH HAZARDS

DRUGS

WHAT IS A DRUG?

A drug is a chemical substance which induces particular effects. When people become dependent on the drug to produce this effect they become drug abusers. Drug abuse causes illness and death.

Some drugs can be beneficial when used for medical reasons under medical supervision. Drugs taken for medical reasons are socially accepted drugs.

BENEFITS TO PEOPLE

Drugs can:
- Fight disease (antibiotics, etc.)
- Reduce pain
- Improve the quality of life during certain illnesses

DRUG ABUSE

WHY YOUNG PEOPLE ABUSE DRUGS

- To look cool and be part of the gang
- Peer pressure
- For fun and out of curiosity
- For pleasure
- To escape from problems
- To rebel against parents and society
- To feed an addiction

SOLVENT ABUSE

Inhaling substances, e.g. gases, vapours or fumes, from a variety of products produces hallucinogenic effects. Some people become addicted to these solvents. Death can be sudden.

Effects of solvent abuse:
- Ability to concentrate is reduced
- Damage to the mouth, nose and internal organs
- Difficulty with breathing
- Disruptive and aggressive behaviour
- Hallucinations

ADDICTION

When a person becomes addicted to a drug they crave the effect that the drug can produce and so become dependent on the drug. They may be unable to stop taking the drug without professional help. Addiction may be physical or psychological.

EFFECTS OF DRUG ABUSE

Effects of drug abuse on the individual:

- Damage to general health and body organs
- Addiction and dependence
- Accidental death, suicide
- Resistance to medically prescribed drugs in times of illness
- Danger of AIDS where addicts share or use dirty needles
- Problems with family and friends
- Addicts may become criminals to feed their drug habit
- Unemployment

Drug abuse not only affects an individual but also affects family, friends, school and community.

Some effects of drug abuse on the community:

- Crime
- Accidental death of drug abuser
- Dirty used needles discarded in the locality
- Drug pushers move into an area
- Many drug addicts lose their jobs because of their addiction
- Unemployment levels rise

Some effects of drug abuse on the family:

- Violence
- Broken relationships, family rows
- Teenagers leaving home
- Crime
- Unemployment
- Illness
- Danger of spread of disease

SOURCES OF HELP

- Health Boards
- Drug treatment centres
- Hospitals

ALCOHOL

Alcohol is a legally available drug. Taken in moderation, alcohol can be socially acceptable.

REASONS FOR DRINKING ALCOHOL

People drink because of:
- Peer pressure
- The need for social acceptance
- To relax and get rid of tension
- To feel more confident and overcome shyness

EFFECTS OF ALCOHOL

The absorption of alcohol is determined by:
- Amount of food eaten before or with the drink
- Quantity of drink taken
- Gender of the drinker
- Size of the drinker
- Time taken to drink

Immediate effects of alcohol on the body:
- Slower reactions and confusion
- Loss of co-ordination
- Mood changes
- Loss of self-control
- Poor judgement

Long-term effects of alcohol on the body:
- Addiction to alcohol
- Cancer of the mouth and throat
- Damage to liver and brain cells
- Depression
- Heart disease
- Stomach ulcers

Effects of alcoholism on the family and society:
- Absenteeism at work
- Crime
- Financial difficulties
- Illness
- Road accidents, even death
- Relationships break down
- Violence

SOURCES OF HELP

Help is available from:
- Alcoholics Anonymous
- Al Anon
- Alateen

SMOKING

Tobacco is used in cigars, cigarettes and pipes. Tobacco contains nicotine and tar and produces carbon monoxide and smoke particles when smoked.

Smoking affects the smokers themselves and people in their company. Smokers inhale the chemical contents of the cigarette smoke directly. Passive smokers inhale some of these elements and this can affect them also.

Smoking produces carcinogens which may cause cancer. Smoking and passive smoking are damaging to health.

REASONS YOUNG PEOPLE SMOKE

- Peer pressure
- To be part of the crowd and fit in
- To appear cool

EFFECTS OF SMOKING

- Smoking seriously damages health
- Children born to smoking mothers generally weigh less than children born to non-smokers
- Smokers can suffer from heart disease, cancer of the lungs, mouth and throat

Pregnant women should not smoke because they run the risk of stillbirth, premature birth or miscarriage.

GOVERNMENT REGULATIONS

The government has tried to control smoking in a number of ways:
- All cigarettes must carry a health warning
- Restaurants must have smoking and non-smoking areas
- The display of 'No Smoking' signs is encouraged
- Work places must be non-smoking areas (in some cases smoking areas are provided for the smokers)
- Smoking is not allowed in cinemas and other public places
- Taxes are increased at budget time

44

TEXTILES

WHAT ARE TEXTILES?

Textiles can be described as cloths, fabrics and materials, which are used to make a variety of items.

FUNCTIONS OF TEXTILES

Textiles fulfil the basic needs of:
- Modesty
- Safety against fire
- Protection against dirt and grime
- Protection against cold, excessive heat, damp, wind
- Warmth during winter

How textiles identify people:
- Self-expression (e.g. by wearing colourful, creative or unusual outfits)
- In sport (clothes worn by athletes, divers, mountaineers)
- At work (uniforms or clothes worn by bus drivers, doctors, mechanics)

CHOICE OF TEXTILES

Choice of textiles may be influenced by the following factors:
- Aesthetics
- Culture
- Good value
- Tradition
- Fashion trends
- Safety
- Employment
- Fabric care
- Finance available

USES OF TEXTILES

We are surrounded by textiles every day. Textiles are used in the home, in public buildings, shops, hotels, places of work and leisure. They are used for:
- Bathroom items (towels, face cloths)

- Bed-linen (sheets, duvet covers, pillowcases)
- Carpets and rugs in the home and in other buildings
- Clothing (underwear, shirts, jackets, etc.)
- Flags
- Kitchen items (tea cosy, tea towels, napkins)
- Parachutes
- Sails on boats
- Soft furnishings (curtains, cushion covers, loose covers, etc.)
- Sportswear
- Upholstery (in cars, buses, trains, planes, cinemas, etc.)

PROPERTIES OF TEXTILES

How a fabric drapes, feels, looks and reacts to wear and tear can be described as the characteristics or properties of the fabric. These properties may be desirable or undesirable. They can then be categorised into advantages and disadvantages of the fabric.

Desirable properties

- Absorbent
- Cool and crisp or warm and soft
- Drapes well
- Flammability (flame resistant)
- Resilient
- Stain resistant
- Washable
- Suitable weight (light or heavy fabric)
- Comfortable
- Crease resistant
- Durability (strength)
- Insulates (keeps in heat)
- Shrink resistant
- Good texture (closely woven)
- Waterproof

Undesirable properties

- Creases easily
- Delicate
- Burns readily
- Irritates the skin
- Loosely woven
- Surface pills
- Shrinks easily
- Stains easily

45

TEXTILES IN THE HOME

USES OF TEXTILES IN THE HOME

Textiles are used in every room for many different items. They are made using a variety of fibres. Textile uses include:

- Bed-linen
- Curtains
- Loose covers
- Lampshades
- Rugs
- Table linen
- Towels
- Carpets
- Cushion covers
- Kitchen cloths
- Oven gloves
- Soft furnishings
- Tea cosies

FUNCTIONS OF TEXTILES IN THE HOME

- Aesthetic (for decoration)
- Comfort
- Insulation
- Safety against fire
- Self-expression
- Privacy
- Warmth in winter, coolness in summer

DESIRABLE PROPERTIES IN HOUSEHOLD TEXTILES

The choice of a textile will be influenced by the function of the item and the properties required.

PROPERTIES IN HOUSEHOLD TEXTILES

HOUSEHOLD ITEM	SOME PROPERTIES
Bed-linen	Absorbent, cool, durable
Duvet	Comfortable, insulates
Carpets/rugs	Resilient, soft, stain resistant
Shower curtain	Water resistant, mildew resistant
Tea cosy	Insulates, aesthetically pleasing
Towels	Absorbent, soft, durable, colourfast
Upholstery	Hard-wearing, stain resistant

CHOICE OF HOUSEHOLD TEXTILES

Many factors determine the choice of textiles. Some of these are:

- Care and cleaning requirements
- Colour
- Cost
- Durability
- Suitability for purpose
- Range of fabrics available
- Advertising and promotion of a particular range

HOUSEHOLD TEXTILES

'Household textiles' refers to blankets, cushions and cushion covers, duvets, duvet covers, oven gloves, pillowcases, sheets, table-cloths and napkins, tea towels, towels and valances. Some of these items are also considered accessories. The function of the item will determine the properties required in the fabric.

CURTAINS

Types of curtain: Full length, short (to windowsill or to the top of the radiator), lined and net.

DESIRABLE PROPERTIES FOR CURTAIN FABRIC

- Colourfast
- Dirt resistant
- Durable
- Easy to clean (washable)
- Excludes or reduces draughts
- Flame resistant
- Hangs and drapes well

- Insulates
- Keeps the light out when pulled
- Pre-shrunk
- Provides privacy
- Reduces noise
- Resistant to fading

Fabrics suitable for curtains are cotton, linen, velvet and man-made fabrics.

BLINDS

Blinds are used on their own or with curtains. Their functions are the same as for curtains.

Types of blind: Austrian, roller, vertical and venetian.

UPHOLSTERY

Upholstery fabrics are heavier and stronger than those used for curtains and blinds.

DESIRABLE PROPERTIES FOR UPHOLSTERY FABRIC

- Closely woven to prevent sagging
- Colourfast

- Hygienic
- Non-slip
- Pre-shrunk

- Conforms to safety regulations
- Decorative
- Easy to clean (spongeable)
- Resists abrasion
- Stain resistant
- Tough and durable

Textiles used for upholstery are cotton (chintz, cretonne, cotton blends), linen, linen union, velvet and man-made fabrics.

CARPETS AND RUGS

Types of carpets and rugs: Carpets and rugs may be looped, tufted or woven. The pile may be embossed, long, short or twisted.

DESIRABLE PROPERTIES FOR CARPETS AND RUGS

- Comfortable underfoot
- Closely woven or tufted
- Durable and hard-wearing
- Resilient
- Resistant to fading
- Rugs should be non-slip
- Stain resistant
- Warm underfoot

CARPET QUALITY

Carpet quality is determined by:
- Construction
- Density of the pile
- Fibre and backing used
- Weight

CARPET GRADING SYSTEM

The grading system is based on the wear and tear carpets will get in the different locations within the home. 'Luxury domestic' is the best quality for halls, stairs and living-rooms. Carpets in bedrooms will get less wear and tear.

CARPET GRADING SYSTEM

GRADE	USES AND SUITABILITY
General domestic	Living-room, TV room
Heavy domestic	Halls and stairs, living-room
Light domestic	Bedroom
Luxury domestic	Halls and stairs, living-room
Medium domestic	Dining-room

FIBRES USED IN CARPETS

Fibres used for carpets and rugs are acrylics, nylon, silk and wool. Wool and nylon are generally blended together in an 80% to 20% ratio, respectively. The properties of both make the carpet hard-wearing. In luxurious, expensive carpets, wool and silk are blended together.

46

DESIGN AND THE WORLD OF FASHION

BASIC PRINCIPLES OF FASHION DESIGN

The basic principles of textile design are similar to the general design principles of colour, line, shape and texture. A basic knowledge of each is required for fashion design.

COLOUR

Colours are divided into primary, secondary, hues, shades and tints. There are few rules in the use of colour for fashion, but seasonal trends influence what is available. Colours can appear warm or cold.

Primary colours:	Blue, red, yellow
Secondary colours:	Green, orange, purple
Neutrals:	Black, white
Shades:	Black is added to colour
Tints:	White is added
Cool colours:	Blue, green
Warm colours:	Orange, peach, pink, red, yellow

LINE

Curved, diagonal, horizontal and curved lines can be used to visually alter the proportions (slimmer) and height (taller) of an individual.

SHAPE

The outline of the garment, which is determined by the latest trends, is referred to as its shape.

TEXTURE

Texture is the softness or crispness or hardness of a fabric. The fibre and the type of weave determines the texture of a fabric. Loosely woven fabrics tend to be soft, tightly woven fabrics are firmer.

VISUAL PRINCIPLES OF FASHION DESIGN

Balance, emphasis and proportion are important visual design principles associated with fashion design.

Note: These have already been looked at under Design in the Home.

PRACTICAL PRINCIPLES OF FASHION DESIGN

As well as the basic and visual principles, fashion design must consider practical factors such as comfort, care, safety and suitability for the purpose.

THE DESIGN PROCESS

The designer must apply the principles of good design when following the design process. The design process is a problem-solving approach which can be used in textile design and other areas of design (e.g. interior design, meal planning).

SUMMARY OF THE DESIGN PROCESS

The steps involved are:
- Design brief is received
- Analysis of the design brief
- Researching possible solutions
- Considering resources available
- Selecting one solution and creating a proposal
- Making a plan
- Implementing the plan (making the item)

- Evaluating the results
- Modifying the solution and plan for the next time

THE FASHION INDUSTRY

WHAT IS FASHION?

Fashion can be described as the prevailing popular style in clothing, footwear, soft furnishings and various other items.

WHAT ARE FASHION FADS?

This is the latest trend or craze, which is generally popular for a short period of time (e.g. platform shoes and boots).

WHAT ARE FASHION TRENDS?

Fashion trends are the latest changes in fashion styles for the next season or collection (swimwear, winter collections, etc.)

WHAT IS A COUTURIER?

Professional dress designers are called couturiers. Their collections are shown twice a year at the major fashion centres.

WHAT IS HAUTE COUTURE?

Couturiers design and make original designs which are available for wealthy individuals to order during their haute couture shows. Some individuals employ couturiers to create once-off original designs. Haute couture is not available in the shops as off-the-peg collections.

WHAT IS PRÊT-À-PORTER?

'Prêt-à-porter' refers to ready-to-wear garments, based on haute couture design, which are available in the shops. Cheaper fabrics and mass production ensure more economical prices for these collections.

FASHION CHANGES

Changes in fashion trends may occur because of:

- Designer influence
- Fabrics available and new fabrics
- Historical events
- Manufacturing techniques
- Time of year

BASIC DESIGN FEATURES

The basic design features change from season to season and from collection to collection (for example, hems are raised or lowered, neckline shapes change, jackets become looser or more tightly fitted, shirt collars change shape).

BASIC DESIGN FEATURES

DESIGN FEATURE	CHANGES
Collars	Mandarin, polo, reveres, shirt
Necklines	Boat, round, square, v-shaped
Sleeves	Kimono, raglan, set-in, shirt
Skirts	A-line, pleated, straight, wrap
Trousers	Bermuda shorts, flares, pedal pushers
Shirts	Fitted, loose, long or short sleeves

FASHION STYLES

A style is the look created by accessories, garments, hairstyles and make-up. There are a variety of styles which can be created from the latest clothes in the shops and older clothes in the wardrobe.

Each style has a particular mix of clothes, colours, footwear and accessories.

Examples of styles
- Casual
- Classic
- Country
- Executive or work
- Special occasion
- Sporty
- Teenage or trendy
- Outdoor (hiking, mountaineering, etc.)

FASHION AND THE CONSUMER

FACTORS INFLUENCING CHOICE OF CLOTHES

When choosing clothes we may be influenced by:
- Advertising
- Age
- Appearance
- Care label
- Suitability
- Comfort
- Cost
- Designers
- Fashion trends
- Fashion industry
- Fit
- Image
- Lifestyle

Each individual decides his or her own priorities when choosing clothes. When buying, ensure that the clothes suit you, fit correctly and suit their purpose. Keep in mind what is already in the wardrobe at home.

GENERAL GUIDELINES WHEN SHOPPING FOR CLOTHES

Before shopping:
- Examine the clothes already in your wardrobe
- Make a list of what is really needed
- Consider how much money is available
- Know the latest fashion trends

When shopping:
- Buy the best quality that you can afford
- Choose colours that suit you
- Consider the cost (keep within your budget)
- Consider the construction (must be well made)
- Consider the fit and suitability of colour, shape and size
- Read the information on the care label (clothes should be washable)
- Consider value for money
- Avoid buying cheap clothes

GENERAL GUIDELINES WHEN SHOPPING FOR FOOTWEAR

- Do not try on shoes with bare feet
- Choose footwear that is well made and comfortable
- Choose footwear with the occasion in mind (work, school, heavy shoes for outdoors and lighter shoes for indoors)
- Shoes and boots for winter should be strong, warm and water resistant
- Choose natural material rather than synthetic
- Check the height of the heel (it should be at a comfortable level)

Note: Keep receipts in case you need to return the items due to a fault or flaw.

GENERAL GUIDELINES FOR DEVELOPING A PERSONAL STYLE

- Know what suits your colour, shape and size
- Be familiar with the latest fashion trends

ACCESSORIES FOR A TOTAL 'LOOK'

To complete the style or 'look', accessories are an essential part of any wardrobe. Invest in good-quality accessories that will last.

Choose inexpensive fun accessories in the latest colours for short-term use.
Accessories include bags, beads, belts, gloves, hats, jewellery, scarves, shoes, socks, ties and tights.

47

FABRIC COMPOSITION

FIBRES AND FABRICS

Fibres are the smallest strands of a fabric. Individual fibres are twisted together to form a yarn which can then be made into fabric.

TYPES OF FIBRE		
TYPE	**SOURCE**	**EXAMPLES**
Natural	Animal	Silk, wool
	Vegetable	Cotton, linen
Regenerated	Cellulose	Acetate, tri-acetate, viscose
Synthetic	Chemicals	Acrylic, nylon, polyester

NATURAL FIBRES

Examples of natural fabrics:
Silk: Chiffon, crêpe de chine, raw silk, shantung.
Wool: Cashmere, flannel, tweed, gabardine.
Cotton: Canvas, denim, gingham, muslin, organdie.
Linen: Cambric, damask.

Uses of natural fabrics:
Silk: Blouses, dresses, lingerie, shirts, soft furnishings.
Wool: Clothing, carpets, furnishing fabrics, upholstery.
Cotton: Clothing, furnishing and household fabrics.
Linen: Clothing, bed linen, soft furnishings, table linen.

SILK

Origin:
Silk originates from the cocoon of the silkworm, Bombyx mori.

Producers:
China, Japan, India.

Production of silk:
Female silkworms lay eggs on mulberry leaves. The eggs are incubated and hatch out into silkworms. Small silkworms eat mulberry leaves continuously until they get very large (about 2–3.5 inches). After about 35 days, the silkworms spin a cocoon of silk around themselves. The silk is held in place by a gum called sericin.

At this point the cocoons are sorted out. Some moths are allowed to hatch to produce the next batch of eggs and the remaining cocoons are dipped in hot water to soften the sericin and kill the silkworms. The silk threads are then unwound from the cocoon.

The raw silk is wound onto reels. This process ('throwing') makes silk stronger, by twisting and doubling the silk fibres. The gum is removed from the silk and it is then ready for dyeing, weaving and printing.

Advantages or desirable properties of silk:
- Absorbent
- Beautiful lustrous surface
- Comfortable
- Crease resistant
- Drapes well
- Resilient
- Varied textures

Disadvantages or undesirable properties of silk:
- Tends to be expensive
- Easily damaged by chemicals, careless washing, perspiration, poor handling and moths
- Expensive
- Prone to rotting in sunlight

WOOL

Origin:
Wool is the fleece of a variety of sheep.

Producers:
Australia, Argentina, New Zealand, UK, Ireland.

Production of wool:

Sheep are sheared to remove the wool. The wool is baled and sent for cleaning and spinning. Scouring removes dirt, grease, sweat and twigs from the fleece.

The wool is carded to separate the fibres. Long fibres are spun into worsted yarn for weaving. Short fibres are spun into woollen yarn for knitting.

The wool is then ready for dyeing, weaving or knitting and finishing.

Advantages or desirable properties of wool:

- Absorbent
- Comfortable and soft
- Mixes well with other fibres
- Resists flames, smoulders slowly
- Resists static electricity
- Resilient and holds its shape
- Warm to wear
- Wears well

Disadvantages or undesirable properties of wool:

- Easily damaged by bleach, hot water and moths
- Expensive
- Hairy surface can irritate delicate skin
- Liable to pill
- Scorches easily
- Weak when wet

COTTON

Origin:

Cotton comes from the cotton plant.

Producers:

Egypt, India, USA.

Production of cotton:

The cotton balls are gathered or harvested from cotton plants. Leaves and other vegetable matter are removed. The cotton fibres are separated from the seed using a cotton ginning machine. The cotton fibres are compressed and baled.

At the mill the cotton is classed and graded according to its quality and any remaining seeds are removed. Carding separates the shorter fibres. The longer fibres are straightened. Short fibres are carded and long fibres are combed.

The cotton fibres are put through several processes before they are spun. Finally the cotton is woven, knitted, dyed, printed and finished.

Advantages or desirable properties of cotton:

- Absorbent
- Comfortable and cool
- Dyes readily
- Easy to sew
- Strong
- Washes, dries and irons well

Disadvantages or undesirable properties of cotton:
- Burns and scorches easily when ironed
- Creases easily
- Cheap cottons become limp
- Damaged by mildew
- Shrinks

LINEN

Origin:
Linen is made from the inner fibres of the flax plant.

Producers:
Belgium, France, Ireland.

Production of linen:
The flax stalks are pulled and dried and the seeds are removed. The flax stalks are soaked to ferment or rot the woody core. This can be done in the traditional way or using chemicals.

The flax fibres are dried and are separated from the rest of the stalk during a process called 'scutching'. The long fibres are separated by combing the fibres.

Carding, drawing, spinning and bleaching prepare the fibres for weaving.

Advantages or desirable properties of linen:
- Absorbent and dries quickly
- Cool to wear in summer
- Comfortable
- Durable (wears and washes well)
- Mothproof
- Resists dirt and grime

Disadvantages or undesirable properties of linen:
- Burns readily
- Creases quickly
- Damaged by mildew
- Difficult to dye
- Expensive
- Shrinks
- Wears along the creases

MAN-MADE FIBRES

There are two groups of man-made fibres: regenerated and synthetic fibres. Man-made fibres were created to replace or blend with natural fibres.

ORIGIN OF MAN-MADE FIBRES

Regenerated fibres are made of cellulose from plants. Examples are acetate, tri-acetate and viscose.

Synthetic fibres are developed from chemicals. Examples include acrylic, nylon and polyester.

Other man-made fabrics are fibreglass, lycra, rayon, PVC and metallic fibres.

PRODUCTION OF MAN-MADE FIBRES

Man-made fibres are made by copying the production of silk. A liquid is forced through a spinneret and thin silk-like filaments emerge and harden. The filaments are stretched, drawn and twisted. Filaments can be cut into staple fibres or spun using a continuous filament.

PROPERTIES OF MAN-MADE FIBRES

Different fibres have different properties.

General advantages of individual fibres:
- Acetate is absorbent, attractive, drapes well and is mothproof.
- Tri-acetate can be permanently pleated, is shrink resistant, warm to touch and washes well.
- Viscose is absorbent, comfortable, drapes well and is mothproof.
- Acrylic launders well, is durable, light and soft, and is resistant to creasing, mildew and moths.
- Nylon is durable and strong, launders well, is crease resistant and resilient.
- Polyester is resistant to creasing, mildew, moths and sunlight, and is warm.

General disadvantages of individual fibres:
- All man-made fibres are flammable except modacrylic, which is flame resistant.
- Acetate is damaged by acids, alkalis and sunlight. It is weak when wet.
- Tri-acetate attracts dirt easily and develops static electricity. It is not suitable for children's clothes.
- Viscose creases easily and must not be wrung out during laundering. Viscose is weak when wet.
- Acrylic attracts dirt, has poor absorbency and looses its shape when wet.
- Nylon pills. It is uncomfortable in warm atmospheres. Strong sunlight, bleach and hot water damage nylon fibres.
- Polyester is non-absorbent and attracts dirt easily. It develops static electricity.

USES OF MAN-MADE FABRICS

Some of the uses of man-made fabrics are clothes, evening wear, lingerie, soft furnishings, ties, tights, rainwear, ribbons, shower curtains, ski-wear, swimwear, umbrellas, underwear.

THE BURNING TEST

Take a small sample of fibre. Using a pair of tongs, burn the sample slowly over a metal plate. Take note of the burning, colour of the flame, smell and residue. Write down results.

NATURAL FIBRES

Animal fibres: Wool and silk burn slowly and smell like burning feathers or hairs. A black or grey ash remains.

Vegetable fibres: Cotton and linen burn quickly and smell like burning paper. A grey ash remains.

MAN-MADE FIBRES

ACETATE burns with a smell of vinegar and leaves behind a brittle black bead.

VISCOSE burns with a smell of burning paper. There is a white afterglow and grey ash remains.

ACRYLIC burns quickly with a dark smoky flame and an unpleasant sooty smell. An uneven hard bead remains.

NYLON melts and shrinks. It smells like celery. Nylon leaves a hard grey bead behind.

POLYESTER melts and shrinks quickly, producing a black sooty flame. A smooth hard bead is left behind.

48

FIBRES INTO FABRICS

Fibres are used to make yarns. Yarns are bonded or felted, knitted or woven into fabrics.

NON-WOVEN FABRICS

BONDING OR FELTING

Fibres can be bonded or felted together to produce a non-woven fabric which does not fray. The bonding process involves the use of glue, heat, moisture, pressure and suitable fibres. These fabrics are used for blankets, carpet underlay, hats and interfacing.

Advantages of bonded or felted fabrics:
- Do not fray
- Easy to use
- Economical
- Inexpensive

KNITTED FABRICS

Yarns can be linked together using a looping process called 'knitting'. This can be done by hand or machine. Knitting can be thin or thick. All knitted fabric has a stretchy quality.

Uses of knitted fabrics:
Cardigans, dresses, jackets, jumpers, lingerie, socks, sportswear, thermal underwear and tights.

Advantages of knitted fabrics:
- Comfortable and soft
- Crease resistant
- Do not need ironing
- Stretchy and resilient
- Warm

WOVEN FABRICS

Types of yarn:
- Filament yarn (made from filament fibres)
- Staple yarn (made from short small staple fibres)
- Monofilament yarn (made from one continuous filament)

CONSTRUCTION OF WOVEN FABRIC

Woven fabric is made using a loom. The process is called 'weaving'. Threads are arranged lengthways down the loom. These threads are called selvage or warp threads. Weft threads are woven under and over the warp threads to fill in the weave. The way the threads are woven under and over will determine the type of weave.

TYPES OF WEAVES

Some weaves are easier to work than others. Examples of different weaves are:
- Simple (plain weave)
- Complex (basket, herringbone, towelling, twill, velvet)

PLAIN WEAVE (SHOWING CONSTRUCTION OF WARP AND WEFT)

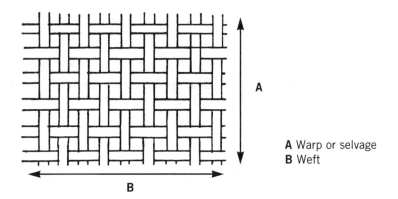

A

B

A Warp or selvage
B Weft

49

FABRIC FINISHES

Fibres are blended together to create fabrics with new properties. Fabrics are treated in a variety of ways to improve their desirable properties. Fabric finishes generally involve a chemical process. Finishes improve fabrics, making them perform better and look better.

When you buy items made with fabrics, the label will provide valuable care and cleaning information. Follow the manufacturer's instructions exactly. Fabrics with special finishes require care when cleaning them.

FABRIC FINISHES

TYPES OF FINISHES	USES
Anti-static	Carpets, clothing
Brushing or napping	Brushed nylon
Crease resistant	Clothing, furnishings
Drip-drying	Clothing, household fabrics
Flame resistant	Children's nightwear, furnishing fabric
Mothproof	Carpets, clothing, furnishings
Non-shrink	Clothing, furnishing fabric
Permanent press	Skirts, trousers
Stain repellent	Carpets, clothes, upholstery
Trubenised	Collars, cuffs
Water repellent	Raincoats, outdoor jackets
Waterproof	Raincoats, tents

DYEING AND PRINTING

Dyeing and printing are finishes that are applied to fibres and fabrics. Dyeing may take place during a variety of stages of fabric production. Printing applies a pattern to the surface, using a dye to fill in or outline the design.

CARING FOR TEXTILES

GENERAL GUIDELINES

When looking after clothes, a few guidelines will ensure that they will look well and last.

- Clothes that are meant to be dry-cleaned should not be washed at home
- Fasten buttons, belts and zips before storing clothes
- Fold jumpers and store flat

- Hang up clothes when not in use
- Mend clothes when torn and before washing
- Polish shoes regularly
- Store clothes in drawers and wardrobe
- Stained clothes should be washed immediately
- Weekly washes should involve separating the whites and coloureds

When storing winter or summer clothes for the following year, make sure that they have been washed, cleaned, dried and aired before folding and storing.

CARE LABELS

Read all care labels on garments carefully. Follow the instructions given by the manufacturer. Delicate fabrics are best washed by hand using a gentle detergent. Below is a list of frequently used symbols.

WASHING (THE BAR SYMBOLS)

 (No bar) Washing temperature 40°C, normal washing action and spin

 (One bar) Washing temperature 40°C, medium wash, short spin

 (Two bars) Minimum wash, normal spin, washing temperature 40°C

BLEACHING

 Chlorine bleach can be used

 Do not use bleach

DRYING

 Line dry

 Dry flat

 Drip dry

 Tumble dry

 Do not tumble dry

IRONING

 Do not iron

 Cool iron

 Warm iron

 Hot iron

DRY-CLEANING

 Do not dry-clean

 Dry-clean

ORGANISING THE WASHING

Follow these guidelines when organising the washing:
1 Close buttons and zips
2 Empty all pockets
3 Remove stains before washing if possible
4 Repair tears, sew on buttons, before washing
5 Separate coloured clothes from whites
6 Sort into care label categories
7 Wash dark colours separately to prevent dyes running into whites
8 Choose a suitable detergent
9 Select the appropriate wash cycle for the clothes

REMOVING STAINS

Before using a stain removal product, try rinsing the garment in cold water as soon as the stain occurs. If this is unsuccessful, soak the garment in warm water with a little detergent. Remove the stain before washing. Rinse, wash and dry according to the care label instructions. If all this fails, use a commercial stain removing agent.

Storing stain removing agents:
All stain removing agents should be labelled correctly and stored with care. Keep well away from children.

Steps to follow when removing stains:
1   Protect your clothing and surrounding surfaces before using stain removal products
2   Read and follow the instructions given on the label
3   Use in a well-ventilated and airy room
4   Do not use near a flame
5   Test on a small piece of the fabric
6   Use the weakest solution at first and increase the strength if necessary
7   Wash, rinse and dry in the recommended way
8   After use, wash hands

DETERGENTS

Detergents are products that remove dirt, dust, grime and grease from clothes.

COMPOSITION OF DETERGENTS

Detergents or washing powders contain bleaches, brighteners, cleaning chemicals, enzymes, perfume and water softeners.

TYPES OF DETERGENT

- Biological detergent
- Concentrated detergent
- Liquid or powder detergent
- Low-foaming detergent
- Special detergent for delicate fabrics

FUNCTIONS OF DETERGENT

- To wet the fabric
- To loosen dirt, dust and grime
- To dissolve grease
- To remove dirt from the fabric

ENVIRONMENTAL EFFECTS OF DETERGENT

Phosphates encourage the increased growth of algae in rivers and lakes. Algae use more oxygen, which reduces the oxygen levels available to plants and fish. Buy phosphate-free detergents.

FABRIC CONDITIONERS

Fabric conditioners are used in the final rinsing water.

FUNCTIONS OF FABRIC CONDITIONERS

Fabric conditioners are used to:
- Aid ironing
- Soften the fibres and fabrics
- Reduce static electricity

WASHING MACHINES

When buying a washing machine, choose one which is energy efficient. Some washing machines also function as driers. When using a washing machine, choose suitable phosphate-free and low-foaming detergents. Use energy-efficient programmes and wash cycles suitable for the clothes. Check all care labels.

DRYING CLOTHES

Dry clothes on a line in the fresh air as much as possible. Inside the house, dry clothes in a tumble drier (check that clothes can be dried in this manner). Avoid putting clothes on radiators to dry, as this may damage the paint or wallpaper and condensation could also result. Instead, use a clothes horse, but do not place it near an open fire, or a gas or electric heater.

IRONING AND PRESSING

Most clothes benefit from ironing or pressing, unless the care label indicates that this is not recommended. Equipment which is useful when ironing and pressing includes:
- Clothes hangers
- Iron and ironing board
- Pressing cloths
- Seam roll (for pressing seams)
- Sleeve board (for cuffs, necklines and sleeves)
- Pressing pad (useful for embroidery)

RULES FOR IRONING AND PRESSING

1 Examine the care label instructions
2 Clothes should be slightly damp
3 Avoid creasing the garments as you iron or press
4 Hang up clothes when ironed, or fold carefully
5 Air freshly ironed clothes fully before storing in drawers and wardrobes

51

THE SEWING MACHINE

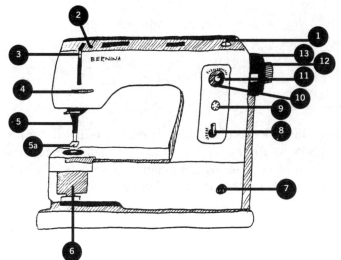

1   Thread holder
2   Thread tension
3   Take-up lever
4   Thread guide
5   Presser foot
5a Feed dog
6   Cover in front of bobbin
7   Drop-feed control
8   Stitch length adjustment
9   Buttonhole stitch regulator
10 Zig-zag setting knob
11 Needle position adjustment
12 Handwheel release
13 Handwheel

HOW A SEWING MACHINE WORKS

Two separate threads are used, one from the bobbin, one from the needle. The machine forms a permanent stitch by linking together the two threads. The tension should be adjusted so that each thread is evenly linked into the other. If the tension is too loose, loops will form. The tension disc may be loosened or tightened to adjust the tension.

BUYING A SEWING MACHINE

QUESTIONS TO ASK

- How much can I spend?
- Do I need a basic machine or one which does embroidery?
- What attachments are included in the price?
- What attachments may be bought separately?
- Will I need lessons in its use?
- Is there a guarantee with the sewing machine?
- What is the aftersales service?
- Does the shop have a demonstration model for sale if I cannot afford the new machine? (Check the guarantee and aftersales service arrangements in this case.)

USING A SEWING MACHINE

BEFORE USING THE SEWING MACHINE

- Learn the name of each part
- Know the function of each part
- Know how the machine works
- Get a demonstration

GUIDELINES FOR USING A SEWING MACHINE

- If you have not used a sewing machine before, take lessons or go to a demonstration.
- Read manufacturer's instruction manual.
- Follow instructions given.
- Thread machine and bobbin in the recommended way.
- Choose correct thread and needle for fabric.
- Remove all pins from fabric.
- Test machine stitch on a piece of doubled scrap fabric.
- Check tension.
- Check that stitch and stitch length are appropriate for fabric.
- Pull the threads to the back. Keep presser foot and needle up.
- Position fabric under presser foot.
- Lower needle into fabric. Lower presser foot.
- Keep bulk of fabric to the left of needle at all times.
- Press on foot pedal and work a row of machine stitching.
- Raise needle and presser foot. Pull the fabric towards the back and cut threads. Finish off the threads.

Never:
- Use the machine without fabric
- Push or pull the fabric under the presser foot
- Use a faulty machine (get advice and help)
- Use the machine in poor light

MACHINE STITCHES

BASIC STITCHES   Straight stitch
                                    Zig-zag
                                    Blind hem stitch
                                    Overlocking stitch
                                    Buttonhole stitch
EMBROIDERY STITCHES   Shell, satin, chain

MACHINE AND STITCH FAULTS

FAULTS   **REASONS FOR FAULTS**

Looped stitches   Incorrect size of needle
                                    Machine not threaded correctly
                                    Upper thread tension too loose

Needle breaks   Poor quality thread
                                    Needle inserted incorrectly
                                    Needle too low when removing fabric
                                    Upper tension too tight

Skipped stitches   Different quality threads
                                    Fabric forced through
                                    Needle damaged or blunt
                                    Needle inserted incorrectly

Top thread breaks   Damaged or blunt needle
                                    Machine threaded incorrectly
                                    Needle inserted incorrectly
                                    Poor quality thread
                                    Upper thread tension too tight

Uneven-sized stitches   Fabric forced through
                                    Feed dog faulty, loose or worn
                                    Incorrect stitch length for fabric
                                    Presser foot not lowered correctly

52

NEEDLEWORK SKILLS AND TECHNIQUES

CONTENTS OF A BASIC SEWING BOX

A basic home sewing box should contain a selection of threads and needles, pins, pin cushion, plastic ruler, scissors, stitch ripper, tailor's chalk, tape measure and thimble.

BASIC HAND STITCHES

TACKING

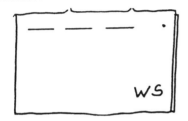

Tacking is a temporary stitch which is removed when the permanent stitching has been completed. Use a different colour thread when working tacking stitches.

Uses:

- Holding two pieces of fabric together for machining or hand stitching
- As a guide for machining
- To hold fabrics together for first fitting
- To hold interfacing in position for machining

HEMMING

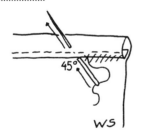

Hemming is a permanent slanted stitch done by hand. It should not be used on hems of dresses, skirts, shirts and trousers, as the slanted stitch will show on the right side.

Uses:

- To finish off hem edges on cuffs, collars, waistbands, etc.
- To sew tapes into position

SLIP HEMMING

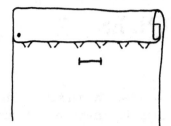

Slip hemming barely shows on the right side of garments. Its V-shape can be seen on the wrong side only.

Uses:

- For hems of dresses, skirts, shirts and trousers
- For attaching a lining to any garment

RUNNING

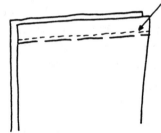

Running is a permanent small straight stitch similar to tacking.

Uses:

- For holding two pieces of fabric together (seams)
- For gathering and making tucks
- As an embroidery stitch

GATHERING

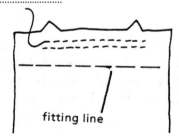

fitting line

Gathering is when one or two rows of small running stitches are pulled so that the fabric folds and can be fitted into a smaller piece of fabric.

Uses:

- To reduce size of one piece of fabric so that it fits into a smaller piece (gathered sleeves, cuffs, aprons, skirts, etc.)
- As a fashion feature on garments

TOP-SEWING

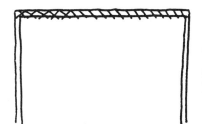

Top-sewing is a small slanted stitch worked along the folded edge of two pieces of fabric. It is worked from the right side of the fabric.

Uses:
- To join two folded edges of fabric together
- For attaching lace
- For securing ribbons and tapes

EMBROIDERY STITCHES

STEM

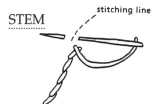

stitching line

Uses: Outlines, motifs, stems

SATIN

Uses: Leaves, motifs, petals

CHAIN

Uses: To fill in or outline designs

LAZY DAISY

tying/stitch

Uses: Petals, daisy designs

LONG AND SHORT STITCH

Uses: Flowers, leaves, motifs

FRENCH KNOTS

Uses: Centre of flowers as a fill-in stitch, single knots or for shaded clusters of knots

BASIC SEAMS

PLAIN SEAM

The most basic seam used is the plain flat seam. It is simply two pieces of fabric joined together with the raw edges neatly finished.

Uses: With medium and heavy-weight fabrics used for dresses, jackets, skirts and trousers

Seam finishes for plain flat seams:
- Edge machining
- Zig-zag
- Pinking
- Overcasting
- Blanket stitch

FRENCH SEAM

For this seam, two pieces of fabric are joined with wrong sides facing. The raw edges are turned to the wrong side and enclosed in a narrow seam on the inside of the garment.

Uses: With light weight and fine fabrics used for blouses, children's clothes, lingerie, shirts and underwear

CREATIVITY THROUGH TEXTILES

DECORATIVE FINISHES

Decorative finishes can be created using:
- Batik
- Block printing
- Plain hand sewing
- Hand and machine embroidery
- Creative embroidery
- Appliqué
- Quilting
- Stencilling
- Fabric painting
- Tie-dyeing
- Fabric collages
- Patchwork
- Soft sculpture
- Crochet

Designs can be inspired by:
- Environment, landscape, sky
- Nature, animals, birds, plants
- Shapes, circles, ovals, triangles
- Abstract designs

USING CREATIVITY WITH TEXTILES

It is possible to create:
- Aprons with interesting designs
- Bed linen with decorative panels (quilt covers, etc.)
- Clothes with decorative finishes
- Wall hangings for children's rooms
- Soft toys for babies and toddlers
- Christmas tree decorations
- Clothes with interesting finishes
- Hand-embroidered household items
- Machine-embroidered garments
- Table linen based on a theme (Christmas, flowers, etc.)
- Tea cosies
- Tissue box covers
- Laundry or beach bags
- Collage pictures
- Stencilled wall hangings or pictures
- Cushion covers with embroidery or stencilled designs

53

RULES TO FOLLOW
IN THE COOKERY CLASS

HYGIENE RULES

- Tie back hair and wear a cookery coat or apron
- Remove watch and jewellery
- Cover cuts
- Wash hands before handling food and after using the toilet

SAFETY RULES

- Follow all safety guidelines given by the teacher
- Know the safety rules if a fire breaks out
- Know where the fire blanket and extinguisher are kept
- Walk in the kitchen, do not run
- Know how to use all equipment
- Use oven gloves when removing hot dishes from the oven
- Report faulty equipment to the teacher
- Do not use any equipment which appears faulty
- Wipe up spills as soon as they occur
- Always cut ingredients away from you
- Take care with steam from saucepans, kettles and casserole dishes
- Do not leave the saucepan handles sticking out from the cooker

GENERAL RULES

- Pre-heat the oven if necessary
- Weigh ingredients accurately and place on plates

- Organise table neatly
- Place used cutlery on a plate
- Keep table neat and tidy as you work
- Place dirty cutlery and dishes neatly beside the sink
- Wash up as you go along
- Return all equipment to its correct place

54

PREPARING FOR THE PRACTICAL COOKERY EXAM

For the practical cookery exam you will draw an assignment at a specific time before the exam so that there is ample time to prepare. Remember also that assignment sheets must be filled out. Some of the assignment and evaluation sheets will be filled during the preparation stage. The remainder will be completed at the exam. These will all be examined by the examiner.

WHEN YOU DRAW THE ASSIGNMENT

Analyse the assignment selected.

QUESTIONS TO ASK

- Is the task a design brief or a comparison/investigation?
- What are you asked to do?
- What factors might be considered? (nutritive value, time, ingredients, cost, equipment, number of people, e.g. a dish for four, season, type of meal, preparation, cooking and serving of dish)

STEPS TO TAKE

- List possible solutions. Keep in mind what you have learned about

healthy eating and a balanced diet.
- Choose one solution and know why this solution was selected. Reasons for choice will be important for the exam. Ensure that you give these on the assignment sheets you fill out.
- Fill in the appropriate sections of the assignment sheets following the guidelines given by the teacher.

BE ORGANISED

- Shop for ingredients. Keep receipts so that you can work out the cost of the dish.
- Know what you have to do.
- Know what equipment is needed. Choose labour-saving appliances when possible, to save time.
- Devise the time plan; test and evaluate it.

ON THE DAY

- Make sure that you have hairband, apron or coat, tea towel, oven gloves, dishcloth, ingredients, equipment, cooking and serving dishes.
- Set the table. Organise the sink, cooking and serving areas.
- Weigh ingredients, put onto plates and cover.
- Ask the teacher what preparation should be done in advance and do this before the exam.
- Tie back hair and wear cookery coat or apron.
- Make sure that you have your assignment sheets at the exam.

THE EXAM

IMPLEMENTING THE TASK

- Wash hands before beginning the assignment.
- Follow the time plan and recipe step by step.
- Observe all the safety rules.
- Keep table, cooker and sink tidy and clean.
- Choose the correct cooking temperatures.
- Do not leave dishes unattended.

- Garnish or decorate the finished dish.
- Fill out the evaluation sheet.

FILLING OUT THE EVALUATION SHEET

Comment on:
- Colour, appearance, presentation, texture, consistency, taste and doneness of the dish
- How well the dish fits the task given
- Any changes which could be made to improve the dish
- How the time plan worked
- Your organisational skills
- Any aspect of the assignment which went wrong at the exam (give reasons why it happened and how it could have been prevented)

PRESENTING THE FINISHED DISHES

- Serve food on a clean plate.
- The table should be spotlessly clean.
- Put a spoon, knife and fork on another small plate. These can be used when the dish is being tasted.
- Leave the assignment and evaluation sheets neatly on the table.

AFTER THE EXAM

- Put the food into suitable dishes to take home.
- Tidy up the kitchen area.
- Return dishes to their correct places.
- Leave everything spotlessly clean.

Remember, there may well be other students using the kitchen the following day for their practical cookery exam.

55

PREPARING FOR
THE WRITTEN EXAM

SOME HELPFUL HINTS

Revise the complete course. Leave nothing out in preparing for the written exam.

Questions given in the written exam cover all the five areas studied. These are:
- Food studies and culinary skills
- Consumer studies
- Social and health studies
- Resource management and home studies
- Textile studies

Learn:

Learn the composition of meat, fish, cheese, milk, eggs, fruit, vegetables and cereals from your food tables.

THE WRITTEN EXAM

The paper is divided into Section A and Section B.

SECTION A

Section A has short questions which students must answer in the spaces provided.

For Higher Level papers, students must answer 20 out of the 24 questions.

For Ordinary Level papers, students must attempt 16 out of 20 questions.

Higher and Ordinary Level students must return the completed answer sheet for Section A to the supervisor.

SECTION B

This section carries the most marks. The questions will take longer to answer. Questions given in Section B cover all the areas of study.

Higher Level and Ordinary Level each have six questions in Section B. In both cases, students must attempt 4 questions from this section.

The extra information needed by Higher Level students is outlined in the syllabus. Higher Level students use a separate answer book for answering Section B.

Students taking the Ordinary Level must answer in the spaces provided. The completed answer sheets must be returned to the supervisor. Section A and Section B are contained in the one answer booklet at Ordinary Level.

TIME

Higher Level: 2 hours 30 minutes
Ordinary Level: 2 hours

MARKS

Higher and Ordinary Levels are awarded different marks for the written exam.

MARKS		
HIGHER LEVEL	Section A	80 marks
	Section B	220 marks
ORDINARY LEVEL	Section A	80 marks
	Section B	160 marks

GOLDEN RULES

Fill in your exam number before you begin.
1 Read the paper thoroughly. Mark key words and phrases.
2 Mark the questions you intend answering.
3 Allocate sufficient time to both sections. Remember, in Section B, four long questions must be attempted.
4 Answer all sub-sections within each question.
5 Allocate time to go over the paper before the end of the exam. Ensure that you have answered the required number of questions and all the sub-sections. Check that you have put your exam number in the appropriate place.

When answering questions, make sure that you know what is being asked and how much information is required to answer the question fully.

KEY WORDS TO WATCH OUT FOR WHEN ANSWERING QUESTIONS

- Comment
- Describe
- Explain
- Identify
- List
- Outline
- State
- Where

- Complete
- Discuss
- Fill in
- Indicate
- Match
- Plan
- Suggest

- Define
- Evaluate
- Give
- Label
- Name
- Sketch
- Tick

Others:

- Advantages/disadvantages
- Benefits
- Cost
- Factors
- Precautions
- Uses

- Checklis
- Effects
- Functions
- Properties

- Classification/type
- Examples
- Guidelines
- Sources

ESSENTIAL SKILLS

LABELLING DIAGRAMS

Know how to label all the diagrams in this book and in your Home Economics textbook.

LABELLING DIAGRAMS

BODY SYSTEMS	APPLIANCES	FOOD STUDIES	SYMBOLS	TEXTILES
Digestive system	Fridge	Food pyramid	Care labels	Sewing machine
Skin	Cooker	(food groups)	Food labels	Basic hand
Teeth	Microwave oven	Where food is	Smoking symbol	stitches
Respiratory	Small appliances	stored in the	Safety symbols	Embroidery
system		fridge	Quality symbols	stitches
Circulatory		Structure of	Fabric symbol	Seams (plain,
system		meat		French)
Reproductive				
systems				
(female and				
male)				

SKETCHING

Be able to sketch:
- Household item made during the course
- Simple garment made during the course
- Kitchen layout
- Simple room layout (living-room, bedroom, bathroom)

UNDERSTAND AND APPLY

Be able to understand and apply:
- Decision-making process
- Design process
- Problem solving
- Management principles
- Work routine
- Modifying a recipe
- Rules or guidelines in all areas covered

ANALYSE

Be able to analyse:
- Case studies in all areas
- Charts and information given

PART SEVEN

EXAM PAPERS

S39

AN ROINN OIDEACHAIS

JUNIOR CERTIFICATE EXAMINATION 1996

HOME ECONOMICS

HIGHER LEVEL

Thursday 13 June – Morning 9.30-12.00

Total Marks 300

For examiners use only	
QUESTION	**MARK**
Section A (total)	
Section B 1	
2	
3	
4	
5	
6	
TOTAL ➡	
GRADE ➡	

INSTRUCTIONS

1. Section A – 80 marks
Answer (twenty) 20 questions from Section A; all questions carry equal marks.

2. *Answer the questions in the space provided.*

3. The completed answer sheets for Section A must be returned to the examination supervisor.

4. Section B – 220 marks.
Answer (four) 4 questions from Section B; all questions carry equal marks.

SECTION A
80 marks

Answer 20 (twenty) of the following questions. All questions carry equal marks.

1. Explain **each** of the following types of milk

TYPE	EXPLANATION
(i) Ultra Heat Treated (UHT)	(i)
(ii) Condensed	(ii)

2. Give **one** important function for **each** of the following nutrients (i) calcium and (ii) vitamin C.

NUTRIENT	FUNCTION
(i) Calcium	(i)
(ii) Vitamin C	(ii)

3. Name **two** good sources of dietary fibre

    (i) _____ (ii) _____

4. List **four** different foods suitable for baking.

    (i) _____ (ii) _____

    (iii) _____ (iv) _____

5. Explain **each** of the following

    (i) Malnutrition _____

    (ii) Refined foods _____

6. Anaemia is too little _____ in the blood.

    _____ is the mineral which helps to prevent anaemia.

7. What information does this symbol convey to the consumer?

   _____

   _____

   _____

8. Manufacturers' leaflets are one source of consumer information.
   Name **four** other sources
   (i) _____   (ii) _____
   (iii) _____   (iv) _____

9. Explain what this symbol means.

   _____

   _____

10. List **four** factors which would influence your decision when buying shoes for yourself.
    (i) _____
    (ii) _____
    (iii) _____
    (iv) _____

11. A_____records the amount of gas/electricity used in the home.

    Explain the term *energy-efficient* _____

    _____

12. Give **two** examples of household waste under **each** of the following headings.

HOUSEHOLD WASTE	
Organic	Inorganic
(i)	(i)
(ii)	(ii)

13. The nuclear family consists of_____

The _____family consists of grandparents, aunts, uncles and cousins.

14. Name the digestive enzyme found in the mouth and give its function.

DIGESTIVE ENZYME	FUNCTION

15. List **four** effects of alcohol abuse on the body.

(i) _____

(ii)_____

(iii) _____

(iv) _____

16. Adolescence begins with puberty. Puberty is caused by a change in the level of _____

produced by the brain.

17. A work routine is essential when managing the home.

List **four** guidelines for planning a work routine.

(i) _____

(ii)_____

(iii) _____

(iv) _____

18. Give **two** examples of heating by convection.

(i) _____

(ii)_____

19. Modern washing powders/liquids are made from a mixture of chemicals.
Name **two** of these chemicals

(i) _____ (ii) _____

20. Complete the table below by matching **each** of the fabric finishes listed with the purpose for which it has been applied.
(i) Flame resistant; (ii) Anti-static; (iii) Brushed; (iv) Crease resistant.

FABRIC FINISH	PURPOSE
(i)	Prevents fabric clinging
(ii)	Makes fabric less flammable
(iii)	Reduces the need to iron fabric
(iv)	Makes fabric feel softer and warmer

21. Name a different fabric suitable for **each** of the following.

	FABRIC
(i) Table napkins	(i)
(ii) Cushions	(ii)
(iii) Sportswear	(iii)
(iv) Babyclothes	(iv)

22. Wool has desirable and undesirable properties, name **one** of each.

DESIRABLE PROPERTY	UNDESIRABLE PROPERTY

23. Give **two** rules to follow when using a steam iron.

(i) _____
(ii) _____

24. Give **two** examples of non-woven/bonded fabrics.

(i) _____ (ii) _____

AN ROINN OIDEACHAIS

JUNIOR CERTIFICATE EXAMINATION 1996

HOME ECONOMICS
HIGHER LEVEL
Thursday 13 June – Morning 9.30-12.00

SECTION B
(220 MARKS)

INSTRUCTIONS

Answer **FOUR** (4) questions from this section; all questions carry equal marks.

SECTION B
220 marks

1. Rice is an excellent source of carbohydrate – this nutrient should provide 50–55% of the total energy intake in order to provide a well balanced diet.

    (a) State the proportions (%) of (i) protein and (ii) fat which should be included in a well balanced diet.

    (b) List **two** types of rice available to the consumer and suggest a different dish in which each type you have listed can be used.

    (c) Name **three** rice products.

    (d) Explain why rice products are frequently 'fortified' with minerals and vitamins.

    (e) List **three** items of nutrition information you would expect to find on a packet containing a rice product and state the advantages of including nutrition information on food packaging.

2. **Chicken Casserole**

1 chicken	2 tomatoes
25g flour	2 streaky rashers
2 medium onions	25g oil
1 stick celery (optional)	Salt/pepper
100g mushrooms	375ml stock

    (a) Examine the ingredients used in this recipe and state, giving reasons, if they concur with recommended healthy eating guidelines.

    (b) Design a two-course menu for an evening meal in Summer, using the chicken casserole as the main dish.

    (c) State, giving reasons, how left-over chicken casserole should be stored.

    (d) List the main causes of food spoilage and explain the conditions that favour the growth of food spoilage micro-organisms.

3. (a) Compare and evaluate (i) shopping in a large multiple chain store with (ii) shopping in a small specialist shop with regards to each of the following:
    (i)   personal service;
    (ii) convenience;
    (iii) value for money;
    (iv) methods of payment;
    (v)   availability of credit.

    (b) Describe **four** techniques used by shops to encourage the consumer to spend more money.

    (c) Comment on the overpackaging of consumer products.

4. Fear is an emotion which can make us anxious and stressful.

   (a) Describe **two** situations which might cause a teenager to experience stress.

   (b) Suggest **three** ways of dealing with stress

   (c) Outline the factors that contribute to (i) a positive self-image, and (ii) a negative self-image.

   (d) Explain the term *self-esteem.*

5. The cooker is an important resource for the preparation of food and it is essential to know how it works and how to use it efficiently.

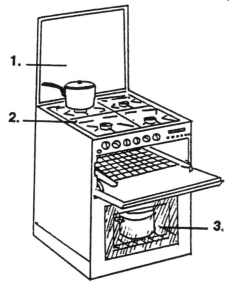

   (a) Name **each** of the cooker parts labelled 1, 2 and 3 in the diagram.

   1._____

   2._____

   3._____

   (b) Give **four** rules to follow when caring for and cleaning a cooker.

   (c) Explain **each** of the following:-
   (i)   Dual Grill;
   (ii)   Split Level;
   (iii)   Thermostat;
   (iv)   Auto-timer.

   (d) How does a fan assisted oven differ from a conventional oven?

6. Using a variety of textiles, you have the task of making an attractive household item suitable as a prize for a school raffle.

   (a) Sketch and describe the item you would make. State the textiles you would use, giving the reasons for your choice in each case.

   (b) List the other resources required in order to complete the task.

WARNING
You must return this paper with your answerbook, otherwise marks will be lost.

<u>AN ROINN OIDEACHAIS</u>

JUNIOR CERTIFICATE EXAMINATION 1995

<u>HOME ECONOMICS</u>

<u>HIGHER LEVEL</u>

Thursday 15 June – Morning 9.30–12.00

Total Marks 300

For examiners use only	
QUESTION	**MARK**
Section A (total)	
Section B 1	
2	
3	
4	
5	
6	
TOTAL ➡	
GRADE ➡	

<u>INSTRUCTIONS</u>
1. <u>Section A</u> – 80 marks
Answer (twenty) 20 questions from Section A; all questions carry equal marks.

2. *Answer the questions in the space provided.*

3. The completed answer sheets for Section A must be returned to the examination supervisor.

4. <u>Section B</u> – 220 marks.
Answer (four) 4 questions from Section B; all questions carry equal marks.

SECTION A

80 marks

Answer 20 (<u>twenty</u>) of the following questions. All questions carry equal marks.

1. Give **two** examples of each of the following classifications of fish.

WHITE	OILY
(i)	(i)
(ii)	(ii)

2. Name **two** foods that are important sources of iron.

   (i) _____ (ii) _____

3. Tick (✔) which of the following foods are sources of saturated fats and which are sources of unsaturated fats.

FOOD	SATURATED FATS	UNSATURATED FATS
Vegetable oil		
Eggs		
Peanuts		
Sausages		

4. Give **two** effects of heat on cheese.
   (i) _____
   (ii) _____

5. Name **two** types of additives which are used in convenience foods.

   (i) _____ (ii) _____

6. Diabetes is caused by the body producing too much **or** too little of a particular chemical.

   Name this chemical_____

7. What information does this symbol convey to the consumer?

    _____

    _____

    _____

8. List **two** principle resources used in the management of the home.

    (i) _____

    (ii) _____

9. Explain **each** of the following consumer terms:

    (i) impulse buying _____

    _____

    (ii) merchantable quality_____

    _____

10. List **four** consumer responsibilities.

    (i) _____

    (ii) _____

    (iii) _____

    (iv) _____

11. (i) Explain what you understand by **stereotype** _____

    (ii) Give an example of stereotyping _____

12. Name the constituent of the blood which:

    (i) transports oxygen;_____

    (ii) protects the body from infection. _____

13. State **two** benefits of FIRST AID.

(i) _____

_____

(ii) _____

_____

14. Explain **each** of the following

(i) **embryo** _____

(ii) **umbilical cord** _____

15. Name **two** methods of heat transfer.

(i) _____ (ii) _____

16. Identify the **two** electrical wires marked X and Y.

X _____

Y _____

Y

X

17. Explain the following terms in relation to design in the home.

(i) **traffic flow** _____

_____

(ii) **aspect** _____

_____

18. State **two** advantages of using a microwave cooker.

(i) _____

(ii) _____

19. Name **two** fabrics made from synthetic fibres and suggest a use for **each**.

Fabric	Use
(i) _____	(i) _____
(ii) _____	(ii) _____

20. State **two** advantages of using a fabric conditioner.

(i) _____

(ii) _____

21. Explain what **each** of the following symbols mean.

(i) _____   (ii) _____

_____   _____

22. Towelling is an absorbent fabric because:

(i) _____

(ii) _____

23. List **four** factors which you should consider when buying clothes.

(i) _____

(ii) _____

(iii) _____

(iv) _____

24. Name the stitch shown and state **one** use for it.

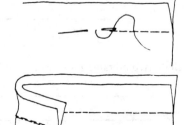

Name _____

Use _____

_____

AN ROINN OIDEACHAIS

JUNIOR CERTIFICATE EXAMINATION 1995

HOME ECONOMICS

HIGHER LEVEL

Thursday 15 June – Morning 9.30–12.00

SECTION B

(220 MARKS)

INSTRUCTIONS

Answer **FOUR** (4) questions from this section;
all questions carry equal marks.

1. Milk is rich in calcium and is an important food which should be included in a person's daily diet.

    (a) Give **two** reasons why calcium is important in the diet.

    (b) Name **two** other nutrients which can be found in milk and give the functions of **each**.

    (c) Suggest **two** ways of encouraging a friend who dislikes the taste of milk to include it in his/her diet.

    (d) List **four** types of milk available to the consumer and suggest a use for **each**.

    (e) Give **two** reasons why milk is generally heat treated.

2. John is planning to buy his sister Miriam her favourite team jersey for her birthday which is in three months time.

    (a) (i) Suggest **two** methods of saving that John could use to save for the present.

    (ii) Give reasons for your suggestion in **each** case.

    (b) List **four** guidelines that John should follow when purchasing the jersey.

    (c) What information would a consumer expect to find on the label attached to the jersey?

3. (a) State the functions of the family.

    (b) Describe **two** different types of family structures.

    (c) Outline some of the changes that have taken place in family life in recent years.

    (d) Describe the role of the family in encouraging gender equality.

4. Water is one of the most important services to the home.

    (a) List (i) the uses of water in the home **and** (ii) the functions of water in the body.

    (b) Describe **two** ways of treating water to ensure that it is free from impurities.

    (c) Name **two** other services provided to the home and state how **each** of these are paid for.

5. Accidents in the home have many causes.

    (a) List **four** common causes of accidents in the home.

    (b) In the event of a household fire, give three points of procedure to follow to ensure the safety of the occupants of the house.

    (c) Name **two** organisations that look after our safety.

    (d) In the case of **each** organisation named, explain how they protect us.

6. The sewing machine is a useful sewing resource.

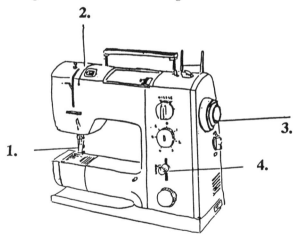

(a) Name and state the use of **each** of the sewing machine parts labelled 1, 2, 3 and 4.

(b) Suggest **two** uses for **each** of the following machine stitches:

    (i) **zig-zag;**   (ii) **straight stitch.**

(c) Suggest a cause for **each** of the following faults:

    (i) **needle breaks;**   (ii) **looped stitches.**